CITY AT WAR

No place like home. The kettle's on, the cups are ready, and with a strip of carpet, lampshade, a radio, and a floral calendar, this Portsmouth wardens' post takes on quite a cosy appearance, despite the biting cold of the 1940 winter.

CITY AT WAR

A Pictorial Memento of Portsmouth, Gosport, Fareham, Havant and Chichester during World War II

Nigel Peake

The News

Published by Milestone Publications
62 Murray Road, Horndean,
Portsmouth, Hants. PO8 9JL

In conjunction with
The News
Hilsea, Portsmouth

Typeset by The News, Hilsea, Portsmouth

Printed and Bound in Great Britain by
R.J. Acford, Industrial Estate, Chichester, Sussex

City at war: a pictorial memento of Portsmouth, Gosport, Fareham, Havant and Chichester during World War 2.
1. World War, 1939-1945—England—
Chichester (West Sussex)—Pictorial works
2. Chichester (West Sussex)—Description—
Views 3. World War, 1939-1945—England—
Hampshire—Pictorial works 4. Hampshire—
Description and travel—Views
I. Peake, Nigel
942.2'62 DA690.C53

ISBN 0-903852-94-4

Acknowledgements
I am indebted to those people who were kind enough to share their war-time memories with me, and in particular to Mr. Goronwy Evans, Mr. Ken Hampton, Major Gordon Kinch, Mr. George Langrish, and Mr. F.T. Mitchell, some of whom also loaned photographs for reproduction in this book.

The vast majority of the pictures are from the war-time archives of *The News* and are the work of former Chief Photographer Victor Stewart, who is referred to in greater detail in the introduction, and without whose skill and dedication this book would have been impossible.

Pictures on Pages 77 & 78 by courtesy of Major Gordon Kinch.

Pictures on Pages 98 (lower) and 148 (upper) by courtesy of Mr. George Langrish.

Introduction

So much has already been written about the second world war that obvious questions arise. Is there anything new to say on the subject? Do we want to dwell on that harrowing period or should we bury the past once and for all? I hope this book will provide its own answers by throwing fresh light on what some may regard as an exhausted topic.

Previous books on the Portsmouth area have tended to concentrate on the major bombing raids which flattened large areas of the city in 1941. I have tried to paint a much wider picture by looking at the effect which six years of war had on the day-to-day life of the city and its surrounding towns from a number of angles: evacuees, rescue workers, firemen, policemen, and the vast number of families trying to carry on their lives in a world dominated by ration books and gas masks, air raid shelters and the blackout, savings campaigns and shortages.

Many of the stories were never fully told at the time, and after the war people were preoccupied with rebuilding their lives as well as their towns and cities. But it was a remarkable, though painful, chapter in the long history of Britain's premier naval port, and a story which deserves the telling even after 40 years. What really did happen the night the Guildhall burned down, for instance? Why did the parents of Portsmouth stage a mass mutiny over the question of evacuees in 1944? What threat — nothing to do with German bombers — almost forced the evacuation of the entire city in 1941? What were the planners' dreams for post-war Portsmouth? Thanks to the files of the Evening News, as it was then known, and the memories of people who lived through those days, the answers are here.

Then there are the superb photographs of Victor Stewart, many of them never previously published either because of war-time censorship or lack of space in the days when newsprint was severely rationed. Single-handed, Victor Stewart ran the tiny photographic department of the then Portsmouth Evening News throughout the war, capturing a unique record of civilian and Service life. Shortly before D-Day, he was among a group of journalists called to London to be told that they were being seconded to various forces — in his case, the Americans — and his U.S. war correspondent's uniform has now been presented to Portsmouth's D-Day Museum by his family.

He was in the true tradition of journalists who lived for and with the job, and when the air attacks on Portsmouth were at their height, he safeguarded his ever-growing collection of glass negatives by moving them from the threatened Evening News building in the heart of the city to his home on Portsdown Hill. Sadly, he died in 1961 after taking early retirement through ill health, with the vast majority of those historic photographs still unpublished. But his pictures, with their talent for capturing the human face of a city at war, have survived as a superb testament to his professionalism and skill, as well as an invaluable record of a momentous period.

Throughout it all, the paper never missed a day's publication. In the event of bomb damage, there were emergency plans to move to an auxiliary printing plant which had been specially built at Rowlands Castle, but as it happened, the buildings in Stanhope Road escaped the air raids almost unscathed. The biggest test came after the fire blitz of January 10, 1941, when the process department was deluged with earth and other debris after a high explosive bomb hit the adjoining railway line. Fortunately, the company had prepared for the worst by installing a private independent power supply for the foundry, presses, and linotype machines. Staff reported for duty as usual, the composing room was cleared of rubble, and the paper appeared as usual during the early afternoon of January 11. It was one of the few local services to function without interruption.

Into the Blackout

One day they were simply children. The next they were evacuees. Before the first air raid siren had sounded, a new word had entered the language, and by the time the war was only a few weeks old, more than one and a half million people — most of them young — had been sent away from their homes in cities and towns to what was seen as the comparative safety of the countryside.

It was a bewildering time for youngsters who suddenly found themselves neatly labelled like so many human packages, and carrying a strange device called a gas mask in a small cardboard box. These were the jittery days when everyone expected that war would mean an immediate rain of fury from the skies, and when the nation seemed obsessed with the idea that chemical attacks were imminent. For the children of Portsmouth and its surrounding areas, the exodus had begun in the tense weeks immediately before the outbreak of hostilities. When Prime Minister Neville Chamberlain broadcast to the nation on the Sunday morning of September 3, 1939, to announce that we were at war with Germany, more than 12,000 boys and girls were already settling into their new homes, some more happily than others. They had gone by steamer to the Isle of Wight, by train to Winchester, Salisbury, or Romsey, or by bus to a variety of villages and towns in Hampshire and neighbouring areas. The lucky ones found a home from home, the less fortunate were billeted on substitute mothers who were far from ideal. London, too, began to send its younger citizens south, and when the first of 17,000 expected evacuees arrived in Chichester, they were reported to be "cheerful and singing lustily, tiny tots and strapping youngsters alike."

The task of evacuation was far from simple, however. The skies stayed empty of menace and the absence of expected hordes of German bombers persuaded many mothers that there was little to fear. They proved understandably reluctant to part with their children and on September 12, Portsmouth's Lord Mayor voiced his official concern at the number of children still in the city. There was an ironic twist to the situation a year later after the Battle of Britain, when scores of children were taken back to London by parents convinced that the capital was far safer than an area of the South Coast which was under daily attack, sandwiched between Britain's major naval port and a cluster of R.A.F. airfields.

But in the early days of that first autumn, before the phrase "Phoney War" had been coined, the accent was on preparation in the towns around Portsmouth and its huge dockyard. Sandbags by the thousand provided protection for the street shelters which appeared everywhere, gas drills were held, and a rash of new regulations came into effect. Probably the most wide-reaching as far as the civilian population were concerned was the blackout, which closed cinemas and theatres, and also led police to report an "alarming" increase in the number of road deaths as cars and lorries, their headlights largely masked, groped their way through unlit streets. To a nation yet undamaged by enemy bombs, it was a serious problem.

In the last peacetime December, 683 people died on Britain's roads. Exactly one year later, the figure had soared to 1,155, more than threequarters of them killed during the blackout and most of those middle-aged or elderly pedestrians. The situation became so serious that by February, 1940, a 20 m.p.h. limit was introduced in built-up areas during the blackout hours, but the Government's attitude was unflinching. When the subject was raised in the Commons, the Home Secretary (Sir John Anderson) told M.P.s that protection of vital targets from enemy bombers must be the primary consideration, not road casualties. By late 1943, it was estimated that 30,000 people had been killed on the roads since the outbreak of war, and the Ministry of War Transport admitted that during the winter, the blackout was taking a greater toll of life than air raids.

Punishment for people who refused to "put that light out" was severe, and householders faced a possible £500 fine or two years' imprisonment for failing to observe the regulations. The authorities faced an awesome task in getting people to observe it, however, and a test blackout imposed on Portsmouth two days after war broke out was officially described as "not good enough." Even when the absence of enemy bombers led to an easing of regulations, with theatres and cinemas opening their doors to the public once more, the blackout continued. So did the problems. In September, 1940, the entire city of Chichester found itself getting an official rap over the knuckles after R.A.F. pilots complained that it and the surrounding area was very poor at not showing lights. The Air Ministry sent a stiff letter to the police, who took several residents to court as a result. One unusual side effect was a newspaper report in November, 1940, that there had been a brisk trade throughout the area in plaster and other remedies for abrasions to thumbs, caused by the continual switching on and off of flashlight torches in the dark.

Meanwhile, Portsmouth's young evacuees had settled into their strange new life, some better than others, and shortly before the second Christmas of the war, an Evening News reporter took the opportunity to visit one particularly fortunate batch in a castle "somewhere in the Isle of Wight." The local council had found that it would cost £1,500 to have air raid shelters built for one of their senior schools, but that for only £100 more they could rent the empty Steephill Castle at Ventnor for eight years. The reporter explained: "As the castle has walls four feet thick and cellars equally well built, the claims of the castle won, and so it has become the chief school in the district." The wine cellar became an air raid shelter, the timbered banqueting hall a cloakroom, and children got their lunches for a grand total of one shilling a week, cooked by a man and his wife who in peacetime ran a high class hotel.

Readers were told that "visitors from other communal feeding centres have been amazed at these lunches, but when they have compared notes they have usually found it is mainly a matter of overheads. At this school, brightly coloured linoleum replaces tablecloths (laundry saved), enamel ware replaces crockery (cost of breakages saved), and each child does its own washing up (labour saved)." There was even talk of secret passages hidden behind the panelling and of haunted corridors. It all sounded like something straight out of an Enid Blyton story.

The sense of adventure soon wore off, however, and by the summer of 1944, with the Allies pushing the Germans back into France and the danger of bombing raids receding, the clamour grew for the youngsters to be allowed home. The authorities found themselves with a full-scale "mutiny" by parents and evacuees on their hands when it was announced that children could still not return because Portsmouth City Council refused to move out of schools which it had taken over as municipal departments. Six mothers placed an advertisement in the Evening News inviting other parents to get in touch with them, and the response was so overwhelming that when a meeting was held in Wesley Hall, the gallery had to be opened to accommodate the crush of people. Their demand — and it was a demand, not a request — was simple: bring back our children.

One speaker pointed out that pupils of the Northern and Southern Secondary Schools, and the Junior Technical School, had been away for three, four, or five years. Many had lost their fathers as a result of enemy action, and an increasing number of bereaved mothers wanted their children at home for company now that the state of emergency had passed. One man told the meeting caustically: "If we have to wait until Portsmouth is rebuilt and council officers are properly rehoused, the children who went away in 1939 may be lining up for their old-age pensions before anything is done." There was a stir when a prefect from the Southern Secondary School, evacuated to Brockenhurst in the New Forest, revealed that their war-time home was "a rickety construction of wood and tarpaulin" where the stoves gave out no heat, and where a master and several boys had been made unconscious by gas on one occasion. "Why should we be kept there under those conditions by the decision of a few officious and bumptious councillors?" he demanded. After a master at the school backed up the boy's report as totally true, a mother shouted: "We will have our boys home, won't we parents?" and was answered by loud cries of "Yes!"

Within a week, Hampshire Education Committee was raising no objection to the return of Gosport High School, but the problem in Portsmouth was not so easily solved. The Brockenhurst debate rumbled on, with the headmaster claiming that the meeting had been given a false impression of conditions there, and 76 senior boys replying by sending a letter which maintained that everything the prefect had said was true. When the Government announced on October 28 that evacuees all along the South Coast could return home, the campaign intensified, and another mass meeting decided overwhelmingly that parents would refuse to send their children back to evacuation areas after the Christmas holiday. By the end of November, the chairman of the Education Committee told a public meeting amid applause that Portsmouth's secondary schools would reopen after Christmas. The seriousness with which the Government viewed the issue was shown by the fact that the Minister of Education (Mr. R.A. Butler) was present at the meeting, and told parents amid laughter that he had thought he was in for a stormy time.

There were problems of a different kind in the early days of the war for schools which had not been evacuated. In 1940, West Sussex Education Committee was wondering what to do with children during the frequent air raid alerts, and had rejected the idea of keeping them in shelters "because of the serious menace to health such a practice would be." The shelters had only a single hurricane lamp, no doors or windows, and no heating or lighting. Any schools which did provide lighting had to pay for it themselves. In the end, it was left to head teachers to decide how long their children should stay in the shelters when an attack was threatened.

For many youngsters, those early days brought excitement and a welcome break from routine. Boy Scouts were pressed into service as bicycle messengers, complete with steel helmets and armbands, or as stretcher bearers at hospitals. In two streets in Southsea, six lads aged between 15 and 17 formed themselves into a fire-fighting squad and spent their pocket money buying equipment instead of going to the cinema. During one raid, their leader climbed a gate to extinguish five incendiary bombs which fell in a timber yard near a block of houses, then helped two elderly women to a shelter. Similar youthful squads appeared in neighbouring towns.

Boys who had found a fascinating new pastime in chasing spent machine-gun bullets from German planes or in gathering pieces of shrapnel were put to more profitable use collecting waste paper and other scrap material when the salvage drive got under way with a vengeance. Some of them, it appears, were over enthusiastic. When the Chairman of Fareham Salvage Committee offered a reward for the child who took the most books to school during a paper drive in 1943, one woman complained that her life was being made a misery by youthful callers. On one occasion, she said, she had to answer the door six times in two hours. Another feature of the salvage drive was the appearance everywhere of piles of aluminium in the summer of 1941 as housewives turned out their kitchens to provide material which could be melted down as part of Lord Beaverbrook's drive for greater aircraft production.

It was the beginning of a new way of life. "Save It" became the watchword for the rest of the war, and the enemy was the Squanderbug, a hideous creature of newspaper advertisements who constantly warned the population against the dangers of waste. Most saving, whether of money or material, was voluntary, but when it came to rationing, there was no choice. Meat and basic food went on ration early in 1940, followed later in the year by clothing and tinned meat. There were further austerity measures in April, when Sir John Simon's severe budget increased income tax from 7s to 7s 6d, and put extra duty on beer, tobacco, and matches. Clothing and material was in short supply everywhere and housewives went to extraordinary lengths to economise in every area of daily life. Even so, they were warned at the beginning of 1944 that the demand for gas in Portsmouth, Fareham, Gosport and Havant was much too high, and unless domestic users cut down, supplies could be rationed. This prompted one angry Lee-on-Solent housewife to point out that the biggest culprits were not householders, but offices and canteens which burned lights all day during the winter gloom and consumed vast amounts of gas to keep kettles and urns boiling from morning until late at night.

With rationing came something else the public were getting good at — queueing. Patient lines formed almost everywhere for whatever supplies were available. Sometimes they were forewarned by newspaper announcements, such as those which appeared from time to time to notify the public that fresh supplies of oranges would be available in Portsmouth, Gosport, Horndean, Chichester, Denmead, Waterlooville, Havant, Hayling, Emsowrth and Selsey, with priority given to children, schools, hospitals, and invalids. One problem solved itself in 1943 when some shops found themselves with nothing to queue for. Notices proclaiming "Sorry, no fish" appeared frequently, and among other things which virtually disappeared were razor blades.

The people accepted it with typical British phlegm, although there were complaints that queues favoured "those with most leisure." That must have caused a bitter chuckle among housewives waiting wearily for a few ounces of meat, but they stuck it, and when new ration books were handed out in the summer of 1942, for instance, officials reported a smooth flow among the 90,000 applicants. The trouble arose elsewhere. To get a new ration book, people had to produce their identity card, and the British had never been keen on this particular piece of bureaucracy. Portsmouth's Registration Office estimated that in the first two years of the war, it was called on to replace some 10,000 cards because their owners had either lost or defaced them in some way. In May, 1942, this led to enormous queues, sometimes until 7.30 p.m., but the public were by now hardened to it. As one official reported: "Early on, those in queues were inclined to be restive and hostile, but in last week's queues there were very few murmurers."

There had been plenty or murmurings in the war's first months, when the effect on some food prices had been dramatic. By February, 1940, there were bitter complaints from housewives in the Portsmouth area about the cost, quality, and shortage of fresh vegetables. Parsnips and swedes, for example, had quadrupled in price in a few months for no apparent reason. When a reporter tried to find out who was getting the extra money, he could get no answer. "It seems to be just another war mystery", he commented drily.

But still the public took it philosophically. "A mere woman" wrote to the Evening News about the beef and bacon shortage: "There is no beef in the shops but us poor people don't worry. We can't buy it anyway, it is too dear. And about the bacon, well that don't cause us lack of sleep as bacon at 1s 10d a pound is a luxury. I have deserted the Danish pig for the Scotch porridge."

With all these shortages, the need for self-sufficiency became more and more evident, and at Gosport, a group of senior pupils from Privett Road School led the way in the "Dig for Victory" campaign by producing 21 tons of potatoes from land which was originally intended as a playing field. They even made a profit of £40 into the bargain. Allotments sprang up everywhere as more and more people joined the drive for home-produced food. Recreation grounds were turned over to the fork and spade brigade, and parts of Southsea Common came under cultivation, as they had done in the first world war.

There were relaxations in rationing, such as the 1940 Christmas box from Lord Woolton, Minister of Food, who announced that for one week only there would be an allowance of 12 ounces of sugar and four ounces of tea, instead of the customary eight and two ounces respectively. But when the Minister visited Portsmouth that month, he forecast even simpler living, with less meat. After a 9d three-course luncheon with the Lord Mayor, he told 500 guests: "Anti-waste is anti-Nazi — that ought to be emblazoned on every Service and domestic kitchen." Amid applause, he declared that fighting men would not go without food in order that people should have abundance in this country. He had told his Government colleagues that the civilian population would willingly and deliberately have a little less. As for speculators, profiteers, and hoarders, he would deal with them "remorselessly, ruthlessly and with intense pleasure." This was the Home Front's darker side, where looters, profiteers and racketeers brought their own problems in the wake of air raids and shortages. There were occasional court cases, but the problem had obviously stimulated the authorities into action by the spring of 1942, when the Commander-in-Chief, Portsmouth (Admiral Sir William James) issued a hard-hitting message which was given front page prominence in the Evening News.

He wrote: "Hardly a day passes without decent men and women being exasperated and infuriated by reports of police court cases which are evidence that, though we have entered the most fateful year in our history, and though our sailors, soldiers and airmen are daily giving their lives for their country, we are nourishing in our midst individuals who were so aptly described recently as vermin. They are not only doing nothing whatsoever to help the war effort, but are thriving in sleek comfort on the proceeds of illicit dealings in commodities necessary to the well-being of the people. I do not know why these able-bodied men enjoy immunity from serving in the armed forces or the workshops, nor do I know where they get their petrol, but I do know that this battle of the People against the Parasites must and can be won if the people close up their ranks and take the offensive." Urging all Servicemen and civilians to have no hesitation in reporting "these filthy parasites", he revealed that individuals had recently been arrested for an operation which had raised the price of liquor for men in his command to five times its proper value.

Five days later, the Home Secretary (Mr. Herbert Morrison) told the Commons that the maximum penalty for Black Market activities had been raised from two years' imprisonment to 14 years' penal servitude. There would also be stiff fines to ensure that the offenders lost any profits they might have made. For the majority of the population, however, waistlines got slimmer still and some food became worth its weight in shillings and pence, if not in gold. At a whist drive at Cowplain, for instance, players were attracted by the lure of onions and eggs as prizes, and one Surrey store opened a potato bar in the winter of 1941, encouraged by the Ministry of Food. Belts may have been tightening, but the nation's resolution was hardening.

Anxious citizens gather outside the offices of the Evening News in Stanhope Road to read the special Sunday edition which was produced to announce the outbreak of war on September 3, 1939.

A touch of the old ways as one man uses a handcart to transport evacuees' luggage to the station. Portsmouth had begun to empty itself of young people a month before the war started, and by September 3, more than 12,000 had left for new homes.

All aboard for the Isle of Wight. Gas masks at the ready, another batch of young evacuees ***(above)*** *join the exodus from the Dockyard city. Some were fortunate enough to find themselves housed in an ancient castle, with its own tales of hauntings and secret passages. Others* ***(below)*** *put a brave face on things as they by train or bus for bewildering new surroundings.*

PEARSONS
WHITBREADS ALE & STOUT
SPECIAL
JEYES FLUID

The town came to the country in huge numbers that first autumn. ***Above,*** *children from Gosport are marshalled into their temporary homes at Hambledon under the watchful eye of villagers.* ***Below,*** *these London children, each complete with gas mask, enjoy the late September sunshine in the West Sussex village of South Harting.*

Some children went farther afield — or started to. This lucky group of youngsters are pictured on their return to Portsmouth after the liner taking them and 300 others to Canada was torpedoed in September, 1940.

Queen Elizabeth (now the Queen Mother) visited Bosham in December, 1939, and enjoyed a meal of beef stew, potatoes and jam tart when she joined a group of London children who had been evacuated to West Sussex.

Those who stayed behind soon found themselves contributing to the war effort. ***Above,*** *children at Waterlooville lend a hand to fill sandbags, needed to protect homes and shelters, while Boy Scouts* ***(below)*** *found themselves with additional items of uniform — steel helmets and armbands — when they became messengers for first aid posts.*

Marbles and conkers paled into insignificance beside the lure of collecting spent cartridges and pieces of shrapnel after the early raids on Portsmouth and its surrounding towns. Some of the more adventurous boys became adept at dismantling incendiary bombs until the obvious dangers were pointed out to them.

Be prepared — that was the watchword in the early days of the war, when one of the first tasks of the wardens was to instruct children in how to put on their gas masks. The musical accompaniment was doubtless intended to make it all seem a little less fearsome.

The unnatural quiet of the early days led some schools to reopen after less than a month. These smiling children ***(above)*** *seem happy enough to be going back to lessons at St Luke's School, Portsmouth. Others such as the Portsmouth Grammar School pupils* ***(below)*** *had to wait five years before they returned to the city.*

*For those not evacuated, it was either school as usual, typified by the youngsters at Elson, Gosport **(above)**, or sometimes in new surroundings, such as this class being held in the vestry of Farlington Church **(below)**.*

They seem happy enough — these Portsmouth Grammar School pupils ***(above)*** *were settling into a new routine at Sparsholt, near Winchester.* ***Below,*** *this smartly uniformed group arrive home for the first Christmas holiday of the war.*

War meant shortages, shortages meant rationing, and rationing meant queues. ***Above,*** *volunteers prepare ration books and coupons in October, 1939. The first items to go on ration were bacon, butter and sugar in January, 1940, followed by meat two months later, as shown by this advertisement* ***(below, left)*** *from the Evening News. Three years later, the Government was still busy trying to persuade people that there was nothing like potatoes for variety at mealtimes* ***(below, right).***

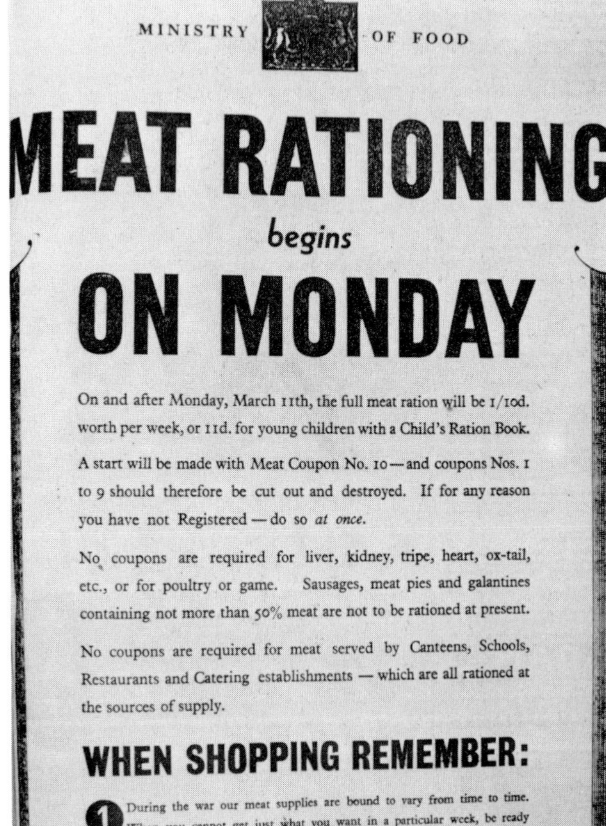

Opposite page: *The weekly food ration for one person was as follows:*

- *Unrestricted bread, cereals, and potatoes*
- *1s 2d worth of meat (7p in today's currency), representing at that time a weight of about one pound*
- *225 grams of sugar*
- *115 grams of jam or honey*
- *225 grams of fat*
- *85 grams of cheese*
- *55 grams of coffee*
- *Just over half an egg*
- *1,185 grams of liquid milk (about four pints)*

Queueing was good practice for these women, pictured in the early months of the war as they waited to make applications for air raid shelters. By 1945, women the nation over were heartily tired of queueing for everything from fish to fruit. Butchers and their assistants ***(below)*** *had to line up, too, for their allocation of offal and other unrationed meat in March, 1940.*

Looking like a tinker's dream, this handcart was piled high with aluminium items when Gosport's A.R.P. wardens started their own salvage drive in the summer of 1940. Waste material of every sort was pressed into service, from books and newspapers ***(below, right)*** *to human hair for making plastic moulds* ***(below, left)****.*

*With every item of scrap becoming precious, these lads at Portchester **(above)** set to with a will when it came to collecting waste paper in a variety of carriers. And even a broken down car such as this one on a dump at Fareham **(below)** had its uses.*

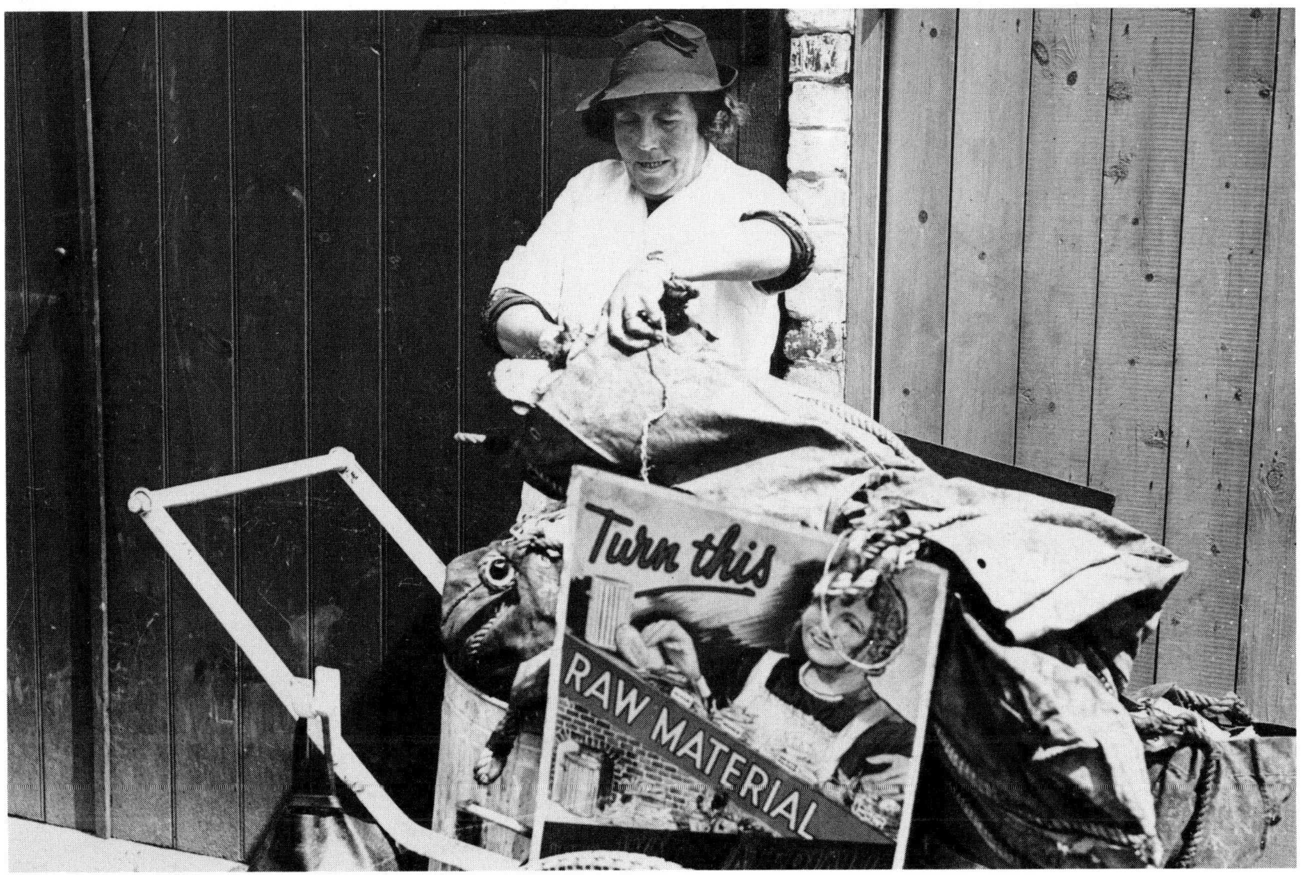

*Public collections became a regular feature of life of town life, from the lady making her rounds with the swill cart **(above)** to this party of W.V.S. women **(below)** on a fuel-saving drive in the winter of 1942, urging householders to use less electricity.*

A first aid party from No. 1 A.R.P. Depot at Milton takes to the streets in December, 1941, in a search for everything from bones to brass, bottles, and books. Practising the economy that they preached, they pulled the cart themselves.

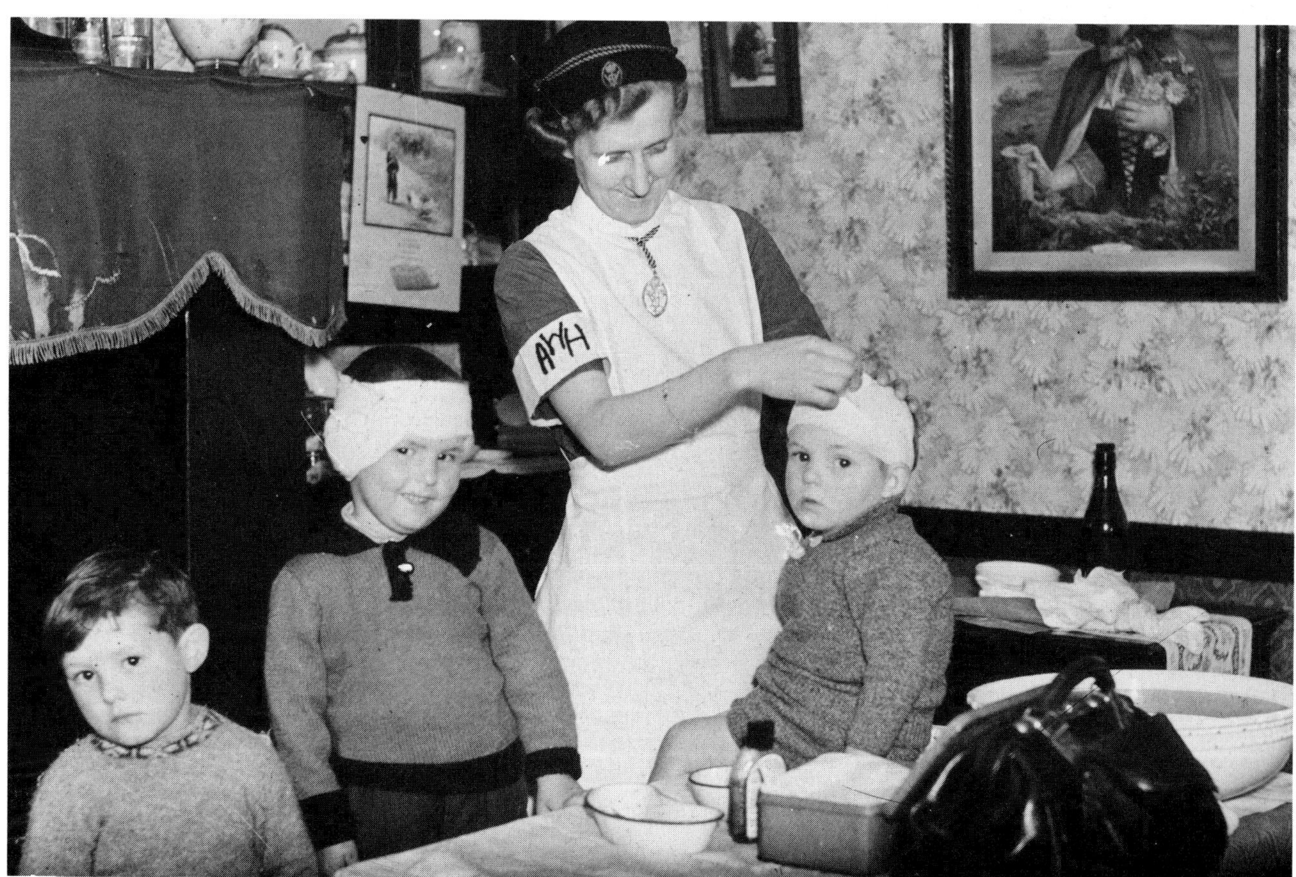

Young victims of a Portsmouth bombing raid get some tender care from a nurse in the spring of 1941.

The Navy did its share on the Home Front. ***Above,*** *ratings lend a hand with the potato harvest, all part of the great self-sufficiency drive to help beat the German submarine blockade.*

Below, *these two officers obviously believed in setting a fuel-saving example with a smart pony and trap turn-out.*

Life in the Shelter

As the ghostly wail of air raid sirens became a familiar sound throughout the country in that first winter of the war, millions of people had to come to terms with a new experience — life in the shelter.

Whether crouching under reinforced dining room tables, making the best of small garden shelters, or joining the neighbours in one of the large communal structures, whole families soon adapted to the new way of living. A succession of pamphlets and advertisements told them what to do when the sirens sounded and how to make their temporary, but frequently used, "homes" more bearable.

The basic model was the Morrison shelter, named after the Minister of Home Security and looking rather like a steel table with wire mesh sides, which was designed for use in the home. Far more widely used was the Anderson shelter, a corrugated steel affair which was erected in the garden, covered with earth, could hold up to six people at a pinch, and took its name from the Home Secretary, Sir John Anderson. At the beginning of the war, about two and a half million were distributed free, but after October, 1939, people earning more than £5 a week had to pay for them. The official policy of encouraging large communal shelters meant that production of Andersons stopped early in 1940. They were so well established, however, that pages of advice appeared in the newspapers on how to make them more comfortable, how to arrange bunks in them, and — most important — how to stop water getting in. Damp was the great enemy, either rising through the ground or seeping between the seams in the curved steel panels.

The Portsmouth area prize for initiative appears to have gone to a baker's roundsman from Southsea, whose luxury shelter was featured in a special article in the Evening News just before Christmas, 1940. After reporting that he had gone to "a little extra trouble at the outset", the paper went on to explain: "Not content with digging down to the prescribed depth of three and a half feet below the level of the garden before putting the shelter in position, he went down another three feet all round and filled in this additional sunken area with loose rubble, cinders, and broken flower pots. On top he made a solid concrete floor and covered this with a slightly raised boarded floor similar to the floor of any living room. Then the Anderson shelter was placed in position." His family did not even have to get wet in bad weather, for the energetic handyman made a covered passageway leading from the back door to the shelter, again concrete lined to stop water leaking in and complete with linoleum and mats on the floor. The shelter itself was painted light blue and white, had electric lighting and a small radiator, two bunks, collapsible tables, and a complete supply of clothing, crockery, and food. The final touch was the name neatly fixed to the door in enamel letters — The Refuge.

Tales abounded of how Anderson shelters saved the lives of entire families, while their homes only a few yards away were destroyed in the air raids which were becoming more frequent. They even played a part in local history in August, 1940, when an infant named Jean Rosalie Whatley became the first baby born in a shelter. Her mother had taken hasty refuge there when she was caught in an air raid during a visit to her sister, and she stayed in the shelter with her baby for two days and nights before being able to return home.

The sturdy little Andersons had proved their worth time and again, but many people still preferred the large brick-built communal affairs. There may not necessarily have been safety in numbers, but there was generally a laugh, a song, and companionship. Indeed, shelter life brought its own problems as Portsmouth Children's Court discovered when a 16-year-old girl was brought before the magistrates as being exposed to moral danger. A policeman explained that she had been staying out until two or three o'clock in the morning, "attracted by the playing of accordions and the gaiety in air raid shelters." She had told her parents she was an A.R.P. messenger.

Three weeks later, Hampshire County Council was discussing the problem of "concerted hooliganism" in shelters at Gosport, where lighting and other equipment was frequently damaged or stolen. One member, who wanted A.R.P. wardens to be given the powers of special constables to deal with the matter, complained that "all sorts of people assembled in the shelters. At times some of them are like Donegal Fair, and appeals have been made to wardens to restore order." The situation had become so critical by early 1943 that a special conference was called by the Lord Mayor of Portsmouth when it was revealed that wanton damage to shelters was costing the city more than £9,000 a year. It was claimed that people had unnecessarily lost their lives in air raids because some shelters were too filthy for them to use, and a concerted drive was mounted to stamp out hooliganism, with the W.V.S. particularly urging women who lived near them to help keep an eye on things.

There were other hazards to communal living, as one Portsmouth man found when he appeared at the Police Court charged with making "foolish and rash statements" in a public air raid shelter. His remarks alleging that R.A.F. pilots were drunk when they took up their machines were said to have so upset one woman that she left the shelter in the middle of a heavy air raid. The magistrates obviously shared her concern, and jailed the thoughtless talker for a month.

As the war progressed, so the shelter schemes became more elaborate. Probably the most ambitious were the two tunnelled into the chalk at Wymering and opened in January, 1942. Capable of holding 5,000 people, they boasted bunks in three tiers to provide sleeping accommodation, and came complete with first aid post, sick bay, canteen, and even a smoking room which could also be used for entertainment. One grandiose idea which came to nothing was an amazing plan which captured the imagination of Portsmouth and Gosport in the summer of 1941. An American, Mr. Chalmers Kearney, approached the councils of both areas with a scheme to construct a tunnel under the harbour which would not only link the two communities but could also serve as a shelter for several thousand people. The estimated cost of £400,000 would be borne by Americans who admired the courage of people in this badly-blitzed area, and at the end of the war, the tunnel would be handed over free provided a railway link was operated. Otherwise, it would be returned to the donors. Debate raged for several weeks but the plan was eventually dropped in mid-August, Portsmouth Council rejecting it by 16 votes to 15, and Gosport by 17 votes to four.

While the shelters were promoting their own kind of community spirit, pubs were facing problems as the war went on. By the summer of 1944, the Evening News reported on the nightly quest for beer, and added: "There is a rush here, there and everywhere as public houses close down before the normal time to the accompaniment of the cry "Sold out." The problem was not so much a shortage: indeed, one brewery in Portsmouth estimated that it was selling 1,000 more barrels each week than when the war broke out. But the low gravity of war-time brews meant that there was little "kick" in a pint, and this, coupled with the concentration of troops in the area, meant that demand had soared. Frustrated licensees were driven to opening side doors and back doors at prerranged times to a select band of regular customers in order to eke out supplies, and the manager of one pub wrote to complain about "poachers" who roamed from pub to pub depriving regulars of their meagre rations.

Elsewhere, people of all ages found themselves thrown together in other areas of daily life. School dinners made their appearance, and by early 1943, more than 1,500 a day were being served in the city's schools at a cost of 5d each (2p in today's currency). For busy parents, municipal restaurants were opened to provide everything from three-course dinners to teas, coffee, snacks and even takeaway meals if you took your own containers. Eventually there were 13 in the city, but Portsmouth's first three went into business in the spring of 1941, at the Central Hall in Highland Road, Eastney, the Winchester Hall in Byerley Street, Rudmore, and St Faith's communal feeding centre in Crasswell Street. This latter was replaced two years later by the largest British Restaurant on the South Coast, which opened at the Commercial Road end of Lake Road and was capable of accommodating 500 diners. Initially, the authorities had their work cut out at St Faith's, described as "a dismal and forbidding place", which had been hurriedly pressed into service after one of the heavy air raids. It was soon transformed, however, its walls painted primrose and decorated with murals of English meadows and Swiss mountains by students from the Southern College of Art. The Central Hall was more fortunate, inheriting cane chairs and glass-topped tables from the Lifeboat Teahouse. All three were officially opened by comedy film star Will Hay, who named the one at St Faith's after himself and received an appropriate gift at Winchester Hall — a carefully wrapped onion.

The comedian's wisecracks and jokes were in keeping with official policy at this stage of the war, when the accent was still heavily on keeping up morale and jollying the public along. The authorities were mainly intent on keeping a tight hold on the amount of information released to the public, and on following the official policy of promoting "an attitude of cheerful courage in keeping with the British character." It was even an offence to take photographs of bomb damage to your own property, as several residents found to their cost. In September, 1940, a Portsmouth doctor was fined for snapping his home, and at Chichester, a woman was fined after photographing a crashed German plane at Wittering. Both had their films confiscated, as did several other would-be photographers.

Gradually, the propaganda machine slipped more comfortably into gear as it became clear to officials that the public were far more resilient, resourceful and intelligent than they had been given credit for. But there were still strange interludes, such as the reaction to the fall of France in the summer of 1940. As fears of an invasion of England grew, and with the South Coast especially vulnerable, a Ministry of Information pamphlet on "Fifth Column Tricks" warned that the enemy might arrive disguised as anything from nuns and clergymen to A.R.P. workers or even Boy Scouts. Far from having the desired effect, this served merely to create more alarm and fuel further rumours, leading in turn to a concerted anti-gossip campaign and the celebrated "Careless Talk Costs Lives" posters.

Rumour was seen to be one of the greatest enemies to morale — and the Portsmouth area had a striking example of the dangers in the early summer of 1942. A balloon from the barrage strung across the harbour area broke free from its moorings, floated across the city and touched an electric cable, causing a shower of sparks and cutting off current. Within no time, the flashes had become enemy air activity, according to the stories which ran round the city, and the pieces of balloon fabric which floated to earth had been translated into parachutists by the gossip which spread. The incident led to an official warning that seeing was not always believing.

The constant propaganda, and the strain of living in one of the country's most vulnerable areas, made the need for entertainment and occasional relaxation even greater. Cinemas and theatres continued to draw the crowds, and there was a special treat when Jack Warner brought his Garrison Theatre to the Kings, Southsea, complete with monologues, sketches, and famous catchphrases. He also introduced some youthful discoveries — a tap dancer called Ernie Wise and a comedian who was simply referred to in the newspaper report as Morecambe. Life, and the making of new careers, went on.

Workmen get busy on one of Portsmouth's many street shelters in September, 1939. Just under a year later, people taking refuge in this one in St George's Square, Portsea, had an amazing escape when a bomb scored a direct hit during the raid of August 12, 1940. Fortunately, only one person was killed.

The first aid post at St Faith's, Havant, gets a protective coating during the first month of the war. Such posts were usually staffed by a doctor, a nurse, and nursing auxiliaries, and the ideal was to have one for every 500 people.

Where there's sand, you will find children, though these youngsters probably did not appreciate the fact that their "adventure playground" was an A.R.P. shelter nearing completion at Gosport.

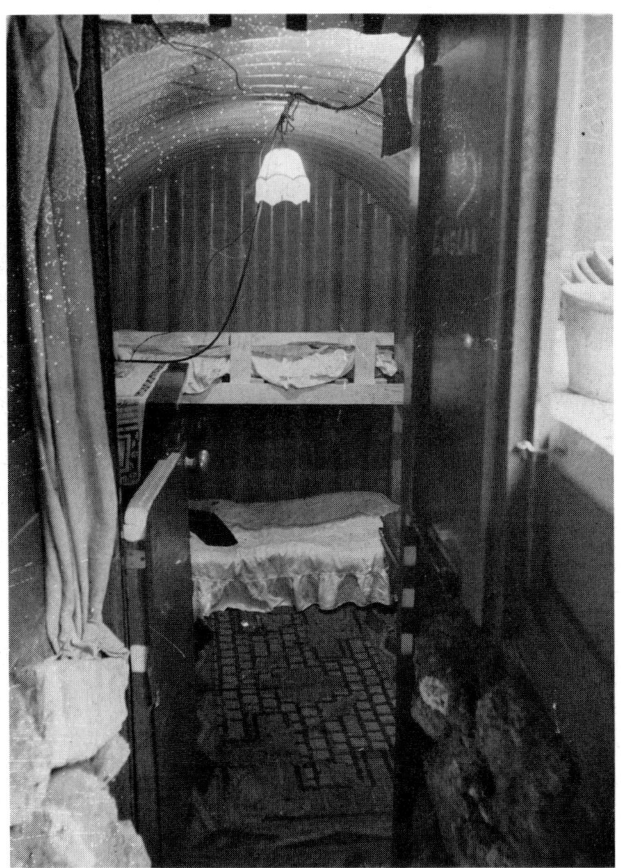

It could never be called a home from home, but at least the Anderson shelter in the garden could be made a bit cosier than the basic model. This one in Southsea, complete with carpet and electric light, was featured in a newspaper article as an example of what could be done with a little imagination.

An A.R.P. shelter takes shape at Gosport. At the height of the war, about one and a half million people were involved in air raid precaution work, most of them part-time and nearly a quarter of them women.

Painted notices appeared on blocks of flats in the heart of the city, indicating the whereabouts of the nearest public shelter and its capacity.

The old police box at Portsbridge took on a new look in the opening months of the war as the entire nation went on air raid alert.

For babies, this all-enveloping affair was the answer to any threatened gas attack. This demonstration for anxious mothers was carried out at All Saints Church A.R.P. post in Portsmouth.

Gas was the great fear in the first months of the war, when the nation seemed convinced that chemical warfare was on the way. Special anti-gas clothing **(above)** *was required for official personnel, and at the Eastern Road depot* **(below)**, *a mustard gas laundry was established for dealing with any kit that might become contaminated by poison gas.*

Out went the lights and up went the hurricane lamps to illuminate road signs for those who were brave enough to venture out during the blackout.

Among the many bizarre ideas spawned by the war were these portable traffic lights, issued to police in early 1940 and seen here being demonstrated in Portsmouth.

Once it was the city's playground, a wide open space for strolling or sitting. By October, 1939, Southsea Common was another military area, the site for anti-aircraft batteries and later a rocket unit. Here, passers-by watch an anti-tank gun drill opposite the Carlton Hotel.

With the call-up of Servicemen in full swing, ratings leave the Town Station at Portsmouth to report for duty on the outbreak of war. ***Opposite page:*** *Men of the R.A.O.C. report for duty at Hilsea (top picture), while others settle in at the evacuated Portsdown School.*

This talented amateur cartoonist found a way to amuse regulars at the Railway Hotel, Portchester, with a bravely dismissive view of the German Fuehrer.

Barrage balloons were part of the city's answer to enemy air attack, and eventually more than 50 floated over Portsmouth and Gosport, the intention being to force enemy bombers to fly so high that their aim would be impaired. This crew at Portchester are kitted out in full anti-gas clothing in early 1940.

Everything looks deceptively peaceful in this air raid alert in September, 1940, but by that time the city had had a taste of the Luftwaffe's intentions, and nothing was left to chance.

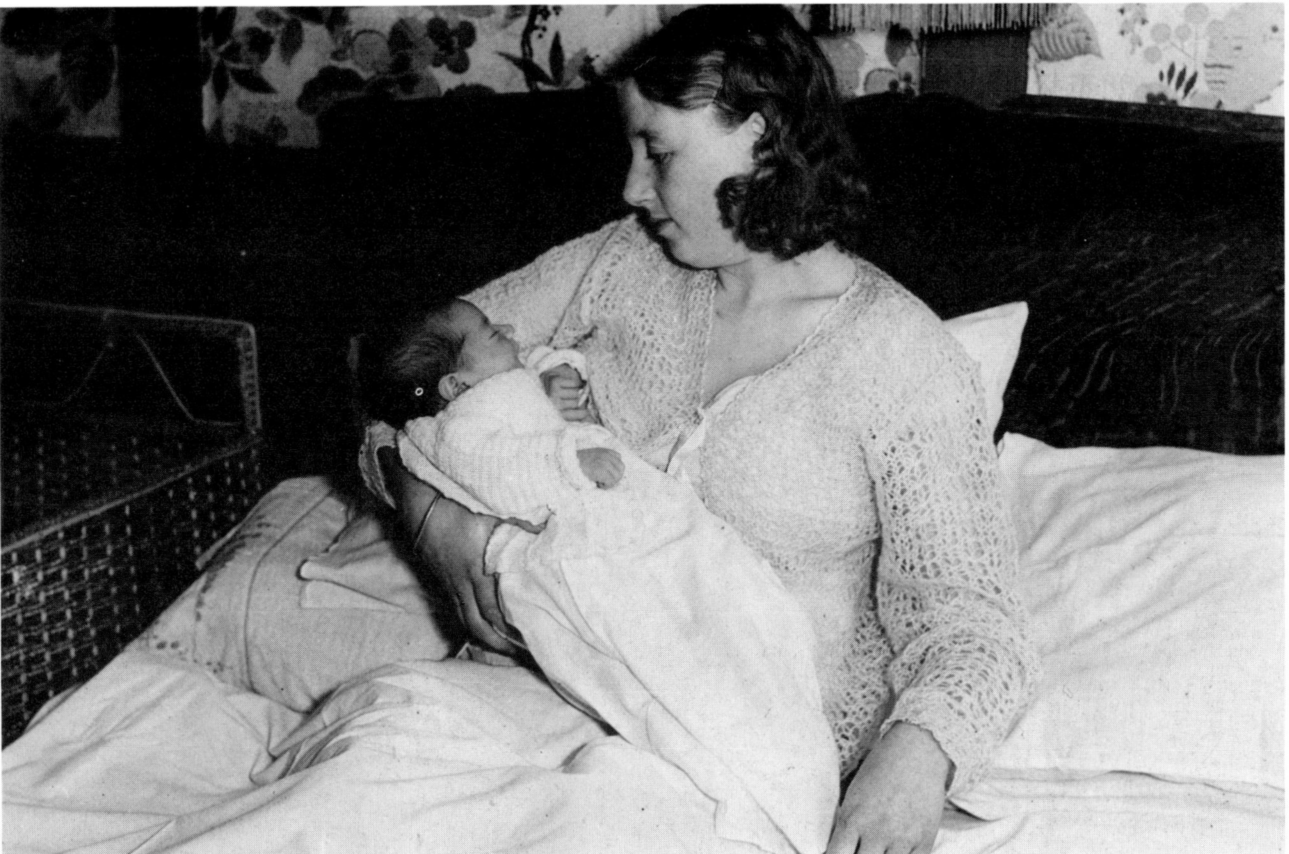

This baby girl made local history when she became the first child born in an Anderson shelter during an air raid. Mother and baby had to stay there for two days before being allowed home.

All clear — the sirens have sounded for the 100th time, the enemy bombers have retreated for a while, and at a shelter in Commercial Road, Mile End, the city's people start to emerge once again, doubtless glad of the black cat on the roof.

Keep smiling through — one golfer found that even bomb craters could provide a chuckle if they were in the right place.

With the invasion scare at its height in the summer of 1940, the sunny Southsea of the holiday brochures became an area of intense military activity. The beach and South Parade Pier were closed to the public on July 4, and it was time for the amusements to go into cold storage.

As the war dragged on, the shelters became more sophisticated. Portsmouth's largest was tunnelled into the chalk at Wymering, capable of holding 5,000 people and complete with its own canteen, sick bay, and entertainment area.

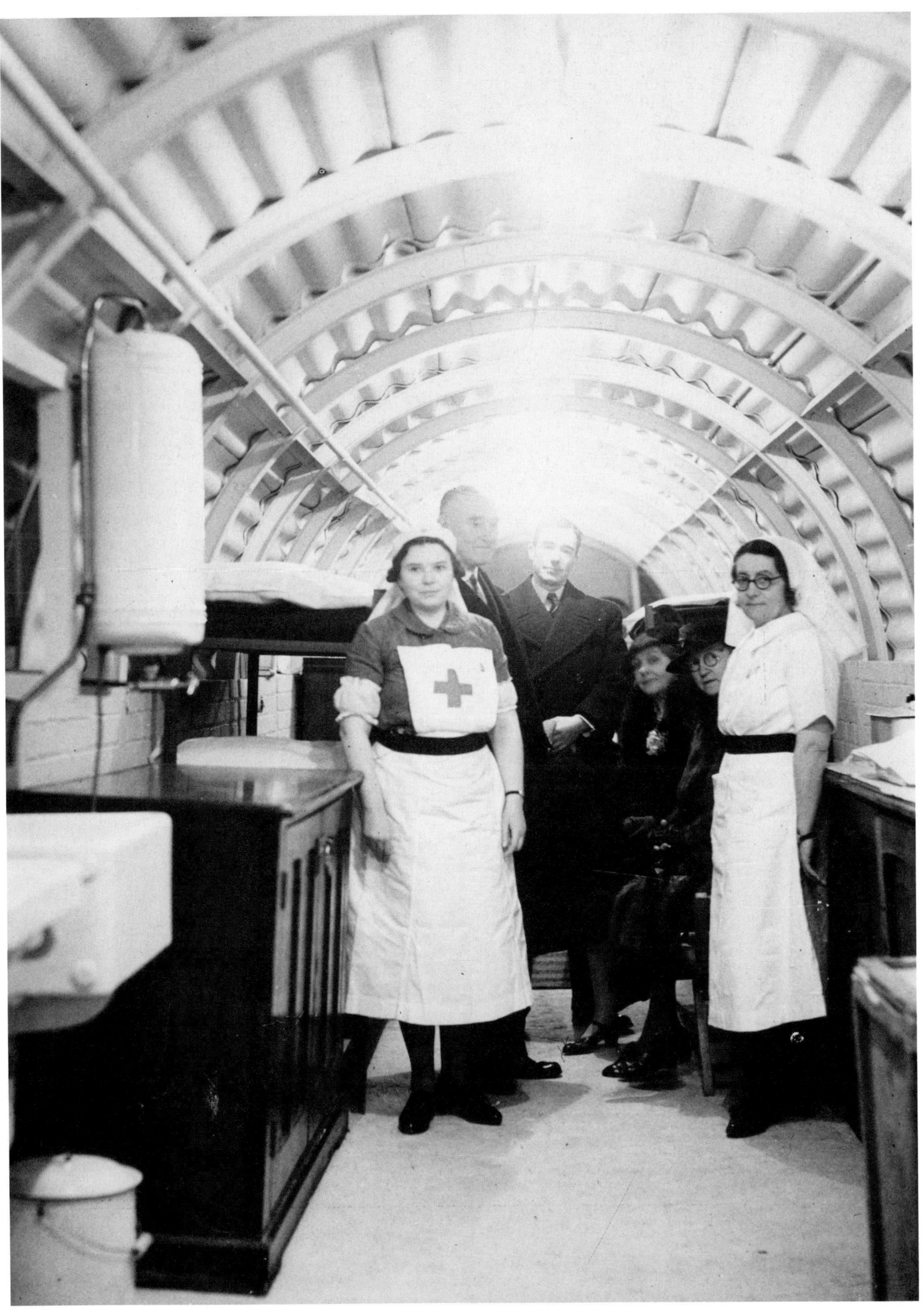

Rations may have been tight, but Christmas still had to mean turkey and pudding for those who could get them. Here ratings at a camp at Hayling prepare for their festivities.

Men of the Tank Corps do their bit outside the Guildhall during Tank Week in 1941.

The huge indicator board outside Portsmouth Guildhall, which charted the progress of the city's various money-raising drives, was torn down and burned by jubilant crowds on VE-Day in 1945.

*Ratings do their bit for the publicity machine **(above)** as they tour Portsmouth during a War Weapons Week. Propaganda played an increasingly important part on the Home Front and produced some of the most famous posters of the war. A typical example was the celebrated "Careless Talk Costs Lives" series, **(below, left)**, part of the anti-gossip campaign which originated in the summer of 1940. Individual areas such as Portsmouth came up with their own ideas **(below, right)**.*

Portsmouth's first air raid casualty was a 14-year-old grocery boy, Jack Whittle, who became the victim of an early dogfight over the city on September 20, 1939. It is uncertain whether he was hit by a stray cartridge from a German plane or a R.A.F. fighter, but he was knocked unconscious and needed medical treatment. Mr. Whittle, who now lives at Waterlooville, is seen here with a photograph of the incident, which war-time censorship originally prevented from appearing.

Right: *Towns such as Fareham might not have been able to match the big cities when it came to money-raising, but their exhortations to people to "save until it hurts" were every bit as effective and valuable.*

Terror from the Skies

Young "Taff" Evans could not understand why his colleagues were staring at him when he reported for duty as usual at Southsea police station on a June afternoon in 1941. Then one called out "Congratulations, Taff, you've won the George Medal." Taff was not amused and told his fellow policeman so in no uncertain fashion. If people won medals, they would be the first to know about it.

Just then an inspector appeared and solemnly repeated the congratulations. This time, Taff bit his tongue and politely explained that he had heard nothing about any medal from any quarter. By the time he was receiving the official compliments of the Chief Constable himself, P.C. 77 Evans realised that they all knew something he obviously did not. The explanation was simple. His lodgings were in Devon Road, Copnor, but somewhere in Dover Road, an official letter lay on a doormat informing P.C. Goronwy Wynne Evans that His Majesty had been graciously pleased to award him the George Medal in recognition of his gallant conduct during the fire blitz which had swept the city that March.

That citation made him the only member of the city's police force to be so honoured throughout the six years of the war, although as he is quick to point out, there were many acts of bravery among the men in blue. The incident that won it for him occurred on March 10, 1941, when bombs rained down on the junction of Elm Grove and St Andrew's Road in Southsea, demolishing a large detached house and starting a fire which was perilously close to a nursing home. Looking back on that night, Mr. Evans recalled at his home at Cosham: "A couple of us had just come in from Palmerston Road at about 11.30 p.m. and had gone into Southsea police station for a cup of tea and something to eat. No sooner were we inside the door than an inspector said: 'You two with the sergeant up to Elm Grove. A bomb's dropped.' Being young, I started to argue and to complain about not having had anything to eat, but we were sent on our way. When we got there, fire had broken out in a big house near the nursing home. You could get through the front window, but the ceiling had dropped and you could more or less move it up and down.

"The blaze was getting a fair hold and they couldn't get any fire units there, so I crawled through to the back with a stirrup pump and started to tackle it. The smoke must have got to me because someone pulled me out a couple of times, but muggins went back in again and eventually we put the fire out. Others may have thought it heroic, but my view was the same as all policemen — you were there, you had to do something, and you did it. That's all it was."

His attitude and his tour of duty were typical of thousands who lived through the city's ordeal by fire. "I remember once we had taken some prisoners to Winchester by train and we were returning by car when we stopped on top of Portsdown Hill. It seemed as though the whole of Portsmouth was on fire — I'll never forget the sight." On another occasion, he and a colleague were running eagerly towards what they thought was a German parachutist, intent on capturing one of the city's tormentors. Too late, they realised that the object on the end was not a man but a landmine, and they were hastening away again when it went off, hurling "Taff" Evans a further 20 or 30 feet up the road. There were similar incidents in the countryside surrounding the city, where "enemy troops" dangling from trees often proved to be deadly parachute mines.

By that spring of 1941, Portsmouth was becoming used to being a city under siege, battered mercilessly by the Luftwaffe's raiders. It was a grim continuation of a year which began unnaturally quietly, but was to test the city and its people to their limits. When the last night of 1940 passed into history, there was none of the customary noise and revelry which had marked the celebrations of previous years. No midnight sirens sounded from ships in the harbour, church bells were silent, and Guildhall Square was free of its usual New Year revellers. Even the anti-aircraft batteries and the A.R.P. personnel on duty as usual at their posts had a quiet night. Gala programmes were laid on at a dozen or more dance halls, but the strict 10 p.m. curfew meant that "Auld Lang Syne" had to be sung two hours earlier than normal. There had been an uneasy lull since the major raids of the previous autumn, when the climax to the Battle of Britain had been fought out over the skies of the South of England. It was six months since the first bombs had fallen on the city on the evening of July 11, 1940, resulting in a number of civilian casualties, including several killed by a direct hit on a first aid post at Drayton Road School. Fifteen bombs dropped on business premises, houses, and two pubs, but the following day's Evening News reported that "throughout the area attacked, Anderson shelters afforded splendid protection and there was not a single casualty among their occupants."

On the morning of August 12, the German raiders were back again causing widespread damage, but they saved their mass attack for the Saturday afternoon of August 24, when the streets were crowded with shoppers. It was one of the worst air raids of the Battle of Britain, with more than 60 bombs dropped and 117 people killed. A direct hit on the Princes Theatre in Lake Road left eight people dead, and this time domestic and public shelters took a heavy toll. By the end of the month, there had been two further raids, mercifully with much lighter casualties, but the worst was yet to come. The deceptively quiet start to the New Year was shattered on the night of January 10, 1941, when 300 enemy bombers made a concentrated attack on Portsmouth, showering the city with high explosives and incendiaries. The fire blitz had begun. One of the very first bombs to fall destroyed the electricity generating station, plunging homes, A.R.P. centres, and shelters into darkness. The impact was so severe that the foundations of the 30,000 kilowatt alternator were shaken five inches out of line, and an added hazard was a stream of blazing alcohol that ran down the road towards the generating station after a nearby bonding store caught fire. Staff quickly manned the pumps and played water on to the wall to keep it cool. Throughout Portsmouth, candles and oil lamps came out, and when other lights reappeared, they took the sinister form of scores of fires which burned from one end of the city to the other. As buildings tumbled and burned, a thousand acts of individual heroism were performed by firemen, policemen, wardens, rescue personnel, and civilians. Three main shopping centres — Kings Road, Palmerston Road, and Commercial Road — were reduced to ruins, and while household names such as Handleys and Knight and Lee's blazed fiercely, buildings were dynamited to prevent the Palmerston Road fires spreading along Osborne Road. In the Commercial Road area, flames raged through the Landport Drapery Bazaar (now Allders), C. and A. Modes, Woolworth's, the Central Hotel, the Royal Sailors' Rest, and two banks, and in Fratton Road, the huge Co-operative Stores were destroyed. The historic George Hotel in Old Portsmouth was lost, and as the raiders swept along the sea front, they set fire to Clarence Pier.

When a dazed city counted the cost the following day, it was evident that Portsmouth had been singled out for tremendous punishment. Huge areas were in ruins, 171 people were dead, 430 injured, and 3,000 left homeless. Among other buildings destroyed were six churches, three cinemas, the Eye and Ear Hospital, part of the Royal Hospital, the Hippodrome, the Dockyard School, and the Connaught Drill Hall. In addition, the city's pride and joy, its 51-year-old Guildhall, lay in smoking ruins, gutted by incendiaries which had started a blaze that burned for more than 12 hours. Days elapsed before the interior was cool enough to be entered. After the war the legend grew up that the Guildhall had been bombed, but former police sergeant Ken Hampton, one of two men on the roof at the time, knows better. "I am absolutely convinced that whatever else happened, there was no high explosive involved," he recalled 45 years later at his home at Drayton. "If there had been, we would not be here now. A couple of lucky incendiaries in one of the ventilators put paid to the Guildhall."

It is a night which has stayed firmly in his memory. Those were the days when entrance to the police force was either as a boy clerk or as a boy fireman in the combined police fire brigade. Ken chose the latter route and as part of his training, was required to learn everything there was to know about the Guildhall which, with its wooden roof, was a recognised fire risk. When fire-watchers on the roof of the Post Office reported "a red glow on top of the Guildhall", he and a young fellow constable called Daysh, another former boy fireman, were obvious choices to investigate. "The place was in darkness and all we had were a couple of torches to guide us. As we got to the bottom of the ladder that led to the roof, so the council's own fire-watching party started to come down with one of their people who appeared to be injured. When we got up in the roof, we could see that they had done a magnificent job. There were sandbags all over the place which they had used to put out the incendiaries that had showered everywhere. We searched all around but couldn't see anything, so we went down again — this was before the days of walkie-talkie radios, of course — and reported to the inspector.

"While we were talking, the Post Office fire-watchers came on again to say that they could still see this glow on the roof. I went up again with another constable and the only thing we could think of was that it might be coming from one of the big square ventilators and that an incendiary might have gone right inside. We eventually located one which was burning furiously — it was a ball of fire. I knew where the rising mains were and we ran out a couple of lines of hose, only to discover — and this was the most frustrating thing — that there was no water. If we had got a couple of good jets of water there, we could probably have put that fire out. We threw in some sandbags, but that was all we could do.

"A squad of soldiers were sent up to join us, because by that time there were soldiers and sailors helping all over the city, but they didn't know their way around and what with the blackness and everything, it was hopeless. We came down floor by floor, with the fire coming down after us. When we got on to the floor of the Great Hall, we could see the whole of the roof burning furiously — I'll never forget the sight. Burning debris was coming down and we even tried smashing the basins in the washrooms and lavatories so that we could get buckets under the taps and form a bucket chain, but it didn't get us anywhere. The frustrating thing was that by the time we were on the ground floor, the water was back on, and when we were in the basement, we were paddling up to our ankles."

It was about this time that someone thought of the prisoners in the police cells which in those days were on the ground floor of the Guildhall. There was the usual night's bag of petty offenders and looters, so a van was backed up to the door, the cells were unlocked, and the prisoners were told to make their way to the vehicle. They were so thankful to be out of immediate danger that not one tried to escape, although it would have been easy in the confusion. Almost the last act in the Guildhall drama that Ken Hampton remembers was smashing the front of a glass cabinet in the police station attached to the Guildhall so that they could rescue the trophies proudly displayed inside.

The aftermath of that night of fire made itself felt in a hundred different ways. So many restaurants and food shops had vanished, for instance, that emergency arrangements had to be made for feeding people. There was even an open-air canteen in front of the shattered Guildhall, with a row of packing cases doing service as a counter. For the various services, it had been a night of sheer turmoil. At one time, 28 major fires were burning with no effective water supply to check them — a cruel irony for a city surrounded by the sea. The city's electricity supply was knocked out for three days, but it took three weeks to reconnect all consumers. Only after the war did the full seriousness of the attack become known. In a speech to businessmen in August, 1945, under the title "Now it can be told", Sir Denis Daley, war-time Lord Mayor, revealed that one of the most alarming consequences was the threat of the city being flooded with sewage. When the electricity supply was knocked out, so were the sewage pumps. On the morning of January 15, the authorities were warned that if sewage got above the safety line, nothing could stop it flowing back into the streets. The

City Engineer had added: "If we get a spot of rain, we are finished." At the last minute, with sewage only half an inch from the all-important safety line, a cable was rigged to a pump and the situation was saved. Sir Denis told his audience: "It is no exaggeration to say that we were within 24 hours of having to vacate the city because we would have been flooded with sewage."

There were countless acts of bravery that night among firemen, policemen, Servicemen, Civil Defence, rescue services, and a host of unnamed heroes in the battle to save the city. Paying tribute to them in a front-page message in the following day's Evening News, the Lord Mayor wrote: "We are bruised but we are not daunted, and we are still as determined as ever to stand side by side with other cities who have felt the blast of the enemy. We shall, with them, persevere with an unflagging spirit towards a conclusive and decisive victory."

They were brave words to buoy up a people waiting apprehensively for the next blow. Four days later, the Lord Mayor revealed the official estimate that 25,000 incendiary bombs had been dropped on the city during the raid, and the city's Chief Fire Officer, Supt. A.E. Johnson, was telling how his men had fought the various blazes until they were exhausted. "The fire service are working as hard as they can to get everything ready for the next occasion when the city may be visited," he added stoically.

Portsmouth's ordeal was officially recognised on January 31, when the Prime Minister, Winston Churchill, toured the city's bomb-damaged areas in company with Mr. Harry Hopkins, President Roosevelt's special envoy. He was cheered throughout his visit to the Dockyard, and one workman who asked for a memento was rewarded with a half-smoked cigar. Just before he left the city, the Premier told its people: "I have thought a lot of you here in Portsmouth, which I know fairly well from occasional very interesting visits over the last 30 years or more. I thought about you and our friends in Southampton a good deal a few weeks ago, when we knew how heavily you were being attacked, and I am very glad to find an afternoon to come and see you here to wish you good luck, and to offer you the thanks and congratulations of H.M. Government for the manner in which you are standing up to these onslaughts of the enemy. Our buildings, our dwellings may be destroyed, but the spirit of Britain glows warmer and the brighter for the tribulations through which we pass."

Six days later the crowds were out in even greater force, this time for the visit of the King and Queen. As they walked through devastated areas among waving Union Jacks, there were cries from the crowd of the wartime slogan "Are we downhearted?", answered each time by an emphatic "No!" Their Majesties frequently paused to visit the homes of families who had suffered during the night of devastation, and had a long conversation with a party of Royal Engineers veterans, now engaged on demolition work, including a corporal who had not only served in the first world war but in the Afghan War before that.

At the end of a busy day, the Queen's message was: "I think you are a wonderful people and I am proud of Portsmouth." The King added: "It is a grand show and your organization is fine." The Queen followed up her visit with a letter suggesting that the clothing centre should be split up, so that not everything would be lost in the event of a direct hit, and that there should be a club to provide meals for the husbands or sons of women who had been evacuated with their children. Within days, the Lady Mayoress replied that there were now 14 clothing centres scattered throughout the city — many of them underground — and that there was indeed already a communal feeding centre providing more than 1,000 meals a day for a few pence.

These extra precautions were just as well. On March 9, the Germans were back again in force in a four-hour raid which killed six people and damaged military targets, shops, offices, houses, and a maternity home. The following night's attack was longer and heavier, with anti-aircraft batteries claiming four enemy bombers shot down and the R.A.F. a further five. Queen Street suffered severely, the Royal Sailors' Home Club was destroyed, and the Keppels Head Hotel and the Synagogue were burned out. Once again, the electricity supply was knocked out by a direct hit on the turbine station, but power was restored by the following afternoon. This time 93 people were killed and 250 injured, and the following night a further 21 were added to the city's growing death toll.

April became another month of raids, with high explosives raining down through a fierce barrage of anti-aircraft fire and rescue squads once again stretched to the limit. German bombers were busy on the nights of April 8, 11 (Good Friday), 17, and 27, causing heavy damage throughout the city and hitting two hospitals on their final attack. The Royal suffered particularly badly, with a direct hit on the casualty department which killed nine people, and two other bombs falling in close succession, one in the courtyard starting a fire in the administration block which spread across the front of the hospital. Patients were already being evacuated after the first incident, and a newspaper report told how "every time the shriek of a high explosive was heard, nurses threw themselves across the patients in their charge to protect them from possible injury from flying debris.

"During the whole of these operations the nurses, led by ward sisters and buoyed by that inexplicable characteristic peculiar to the nursing profession, went through the ordeal unflinchingly, keeping their charges cheerful all the time. Not one of the nursing staff nor a patient was a casualty." A.F.S. men were meanwhile successfully encircling the fires and the hospital's engineer opened steam valves in the boiler plant to keep the flames from reaching it. The result was that the hot water system was kept going throughout the raid, as was electricity, provided by the hospital's emergency generator.

When the Matron, Miss Edith Keen, was honoured by being made O.B.E. in 1943, she took it as a mark of recognition for the entire nursing staff. "Their courage was beyond words. I shall never forget how they worked, carrying the patients down to the cellars during the raids, or crossing the city with messages when bombs were falling and fires raging everywhere. We never had any lack of volunteers when there was a particularly difficult or dangerous job to be done, and one of the most surprising things was the way in which the quietest little nurses, whom I should never have expected to be much use in an emergency, behaved with the greatest courage and coolness when the danger was at its height."

The constant raids of 1941 prompted an understandable desire for revenge among many people, which manifested itself two years later when the invasion of Italy was gathering pace and a debate was raging over whether or not the Allies should bomb Rome. One Cosham correspondent wrote in the letters column of the Evening News: "I would like to suggest that Rome should be bombed by night as well as by day. Let us give these Fascists the terrors of heavy night attacks, as they so gladly gave it to our women and children."

The city bloodied by war was fighting back, not least the anti-aircraft batteries dotted around the area who now had an added and powerful reason for wanting to train their guns for maximum effect. One man who can well remember those days is Major Gordon Kinch, of Bedhampton, who joined 57 H.A.A. Regiment (T.A.) along with many other former Portsmouth Grammar School pupils shortly before the war, and later commanded 215 Battery in Italy. The school link was explained by the fact that one of the senior masters, R.H. Willis, was colonel of 214 Battery and would send his old boys an enthusiastically worded letter inviting them to join up. At the outbreak of war, the newly commissioned Second Lieut. Kinch was busy first on Southsea Common, then in the Isle of Wight and later at Gosport and Hayling.

After an initial lull, during which they manned the guns complete with gas masks and anti-gas capes in expectation of chemical attacks by the Germans, they began to feel the enemy's pressure in earnest during the summer of 1940. Major Kinch recalls: "I can still remember my amazement in August that year at looking up, seeing Heinkels with black crosses on the wings coming over, and thinking: 'They've come to bomb Portsmouth.'" The gunners' first casualties occurred that month at the Holbrook site at Gosport, where one man was killed and several injured, but the true fury of the storm was yet to come. January, 1941, brought the first fire blitz, and when the raiders returned in March, the attack was so ferocious that one gun control officer reported that "our concrete command post was rocking like a ship at sea." During the particularly heavy attack on March 10, 1941, two bombs scored a direct hit on 215 Battery on Southsea Common, killing 11 men and putting one of the guns out of action. Despite the fact that the command post had been hit, the other two guns were silent for only five minutes, and the following night operations were carried out from a trestle table in the middle of the gun park by the light of a hurricane lamp.

When the raiders returned on April 17, Hayling bore the brunt and 219 Battery's site at Sinah Warren was completely destroyed, with six men killed and 30 injured. A graphic account of the incident was contained in "Roof Over Britain", an official Ministry of Information booklet published in 1943 to tell the story of the anti-aircraft defences. "One of the first showers of incendiaries released fell in a half-circle round a gun site. The glare of the blazing incendiaries drew the bombers like moths to a candle flame, and one after another came over to release its load. More than 30 heavy bombs fell on the fields within a quarter of a mile radius of the gun site, but it was not until later in the action that the site was hit. Two fell among the huts, smashing them to matchwood, and a third landed between the command post and the No. 2 gun, which it put out of action, killing some members of the crew. A fourth bomb blew in the back of the cabin as the crew sat at the controls. They escaped with a bad shaking." The battery continued to engage the enemy until only one of its four guns was firing. Then, with high explosives and incendiaries still raining on the position, the order was given to evacuate.

Hayling had been singled out for attack for a simple reason. The entire area was being used as a decoy to lure German bombers away from the prime target, Portsmouth Dockyard. As well as deliberately allowing light to escape from specially constructed buildings on Hayling, to give the impression that the blackout was not being strictly enough applied, a special R.A.F. detachment in the Kench area lit flares and oil-filled drums to simulate blazing buildings. Needless to say, local residents were less than enthusiastic about the idea, but the authorities, though sympathetic, overruled their protests in the greater interest.

Those raids are vividly recalled by Mr. F.T. Mitchell, of Southsea, who joined 57 H.A.A. Regiment (T.A.) shortly before the war and served in 219 Battery, Cosham and Isle of Wight. On the day that war was declared, they marched from Cosham railway station with fixed bayonets behind a Royal Artillery band to a restaurant at Hilsea Ramparts for a meal. "That night, at the Bedhampton end of Portsdown Hill, we were digging with picks and shovels to make a command post and gun positions, after collecting our mobile guns and vehicles."

After enemy action began in earnest in July, 1940, his battery was moved first to Waterlooville, then the Isle of Wight, and eventually to Hayling Island at the end of the year. They were dug in well in time for the large-scale attack in March, 1941, and were helped in plotting the bombers' positions by the highly secret and experimental radar station on Portsdown Hill, which had been in operation since 1940. "Our guns in the Solent fired 1,420 rounds and shot down four enemy planes. They came again the next night, which was clear, and the larger bombers could easily be seen silhouetted against the brilliant moonlight. They were using a new type of incendiary, which burst 30 feet above the ground and threw out a shower of blazing magnesium."

As the danger of invasion receded, the battle-tested gunners were sent overseas, first to North Africa and later Italy. Their places were taken in many instances by mixed batteries, with girls from the A.T.S. playing their part alongside the men. Transferred from "civvy street" jobs in factories and shops, they were given an intensive training course in the North of England before being sent south to join the front-line defences. Their duties included working predictors, height finders, identification telescopes, plotting tables, and other direction finding gear. One young corporal, asked by a reporter how they settled down to Service discipline, promptly replied: "Oh, there is no fancy stuff here. It is all strictly business."

When one of the groups defending Portsmouth went into action for the first time in June, 1942, they claimed one of four enemy bombers shot down. The young major in command of the battery was full of praise for his recruits, and proudly told how several of them had turned out at top speed with only greatcoats over their pyjamas, and had carried on like that throughout the action. The gunners of another mixed A.A. division guarding the South Coast received a special telegram that same summer when they passed their "century" against the Luftwaffe. Among the 101 "kills" they claimed were more than 20 raiders brought down by searchlight crews.

A particularly outstanding victory occurred when two mixed batteries shot down a Messerschmitt spy plane more than six miles up over the coast in August, 1943. One of their officers later recalled: "We saw three vapour trails approaching over Selsey Bill, got to the instruments and guns and waited for the targets to come within range. They were weaving about and as they went away we engaged them again. On our last salvo we saw one round hit the centre plane. We saw it come down in smoke — it dived straight down. We stopped firing because the Spitfires were closing in, and they shot down one of the escorting planes." For their efforts, members of the battery were presented with pieces of the German plane's fuselage by General Sir Frederick Pile, General Officer Commander-in-Chief of A.A. Command. At the same time, the area around Portsmouth suffered its heaviest air raid for more than a year, with an estimated 25 bombers and fighters attacking around midnight on August 15. Six were shot down, one of them crashing in the sea in flames at Hayling, but there were heavy casualties and it meant another busy night for the National Fire Service and rescue services.

For 18 months, there was a comparative lull in enemy attacks, but as preparations began in earnest for the D-Day invasion in 1944, the South found itself once again a favourite target for the Luftwaffe. Hundreds of thousands of troops were crowding into the coastal area, which became one vast armed camp as convoys of vehicles piled up in suburban streets and country lanes leading to the embarkation points in Portsmouth. The whole of the coast from the Wash to Land's End, for ten miles inland, became a prohibited area except for residents, troops, or Government officials. Spot checks on the public were carried out by military and civil police at stations, bus stops, hotels, blocks of flats, and places of amusements, and a growing number of people began to appear before magistrates for not carrying their identity cards. At Fareham, two London women who were said to have been following troops from camp to camp were each jailed for a month's hard labour for being in a prohibited area.

At the end of April, 1944, German planes bombed Portsmouth and the surrounding area, but the raiders met such a stiff anti-aircraft barrage, joined by the rocket battery on Southsea Common, that they dropped most of their bombs either in the sea or the open countryside, and fortunately casualties were few. A number of people were killed, however, when explosives destroyed two air raid shelters. The raiders were back in force the following month for a concentrated attack, but this time six of them were shot down. The Luftwaffe lost a further six later in May, when a large force of bombers caused considerable further damage.

Just along the coast, Chichester suffered a particularly distressing incident on May 11 when a crippled American bomber crashed, killing a 14-year-old girl who was working in a laundry and injuring more than 20 people. The pilot had ordered the crew to bale out over Bognor Regis when fire broke out in the bomb rack, and had set the plane on course to crash into the sea before dropping through the escape hatch himself. A contemporary account related how "the fire spread, however, and eye witnesses in the area were horrified to see the aircraft turn in a semi-circle away from the sea, banking steeply as it neared the Chichester area. Over the centre of the town, the pilotless plane struck the roof of a garage, finally pancaking on to an allotment estate behind Whyke Lane." It bounced on before crashing into the laundry and exploding, damaging some 200 properties in the process.

Throughout the area, the relentless build-up of materials and men continued. Once the momentous date of June 6, 1944, had arrived and the Allied invasion force crossed the Channel to establish a beach-head on the French coast, German prisoners began to appear on their way through Gosport and Portsmouth, some in the blue battledress of paratroopers, others in the more familiar field grey. Other German "visitors" made their debut in far more chilling fashion on June 15, when what were described in the newspapers as "radio-controlled glider bombs" appeared over southern England. The V1 flying bombs, or "doodlebugs" as they were dubbed, had arrived, a deadly device which caused widespread damage and loss of life in London until anti-aircraft batteries and R.A.F. pilots had perfected special techniques for shooting them down.

As they increased, so did the public's anger at this latest menace, and at the end of July, a group of Fareham residents started a petition to the Government demanding immediate reprisals for the attacks. They urged the destruction of a town or village in the Reich for every day the flying bombs continued, and added: "In this way, we hope to make the continued murder of civilians, chiefly women, children and old people, unprofitable to the Huns." The Editor of the Evening News published their letter, but added a footnote pointing out that he could not agree with it as the Government's policy was to hit Germany's military machine, not to enter into a reprisal competition. What the public did not know at the time was that arrangements had been made to evacuate the entire city if necessary. In a top secret discussion with the Regional Commissioner at the beginning of the year, the Lord Mayor, Sir Denis Daley, had been told that intelligence reports showed the existence of ramps nearing completion in Normandy and designed to launch ten-ton bombs, one every five minutes day and night, directed on Portsmouth. The success of the D-Day landings meant that these sites were overrun before they could come into use. Field Marshal Bernard Montgomery, an old friend of the city, had sent Sir Denis a personal letter to say: "You will be pleased to know that we have had a resounding victory in Normandy which will have, as far as you are concerned, far-reaching effects."

Thankfully, there were lighter moments amid the hardship. One incident which caused a stir locally in that hectic summer was the appearance at Littlehampton Magistrates Court in August of a judge who was also a Home Guard officer. He was fined five shillings for bathing in a prohibited area. Among 26 other people similarly brought to the court's attention were "Crazy Gang" comedians Nervo and Knox, who lived in the area. As the Allied invasion forces pushed deeper into France, however, the authorities at home started to relax a little, and at the end of the month, the ban on visits to the South Coast and the Isle of Wight was officially lifted, apart from a few mined beaches. Anyone looking forward to a late holiday, however, was liable to disappointment. Portsmouth's Chief Constable (Mr. A.C. West) told a reporter: "You can take it from me there is practically no accommodation obtainable. The hotels are full and the few boarding houses that are functioning or have not been blitzed are booked up." Even so, thousands of people took the opportunity to renew acquaintance with the seaside or with relatives, and on the first weekend after the ban was lifted, beaches at Hayling and Southsea took on a pre-war appearance and ferries to the Isle of Wight were as crowded as troopships.

Within weeks, the cruelly blitzed shopping centre at Southsea was sharing in the revival, with the streets full of crowds, estate agents selling property again for the first time in years, and housewives patiently queueing for a variety of items which seemed to have reappeared from exile, such as pot scourers, potato peelers, dish mops, and utility china. In the midst of destruction, and after five long, hard years of war, the people of the South once more dared look to the future.

A sight that was to become heartbreakingly familiar throughout Portsmouth as bombed-out families, salvaging what they could from the wreckage of their homes, left for what they hoped would be safer accommodation.

Hit during the second raid on Portsmouth, the Harbour Station was the first Southern Railway station to suffer at the hands of the enemy, on August 12, 1940. A major fire broke out and gave salvage squads a strenuous time.

The worst of the 1940 air raids on Portsmouth — and one of the worst of the Battle of Britain — occurred on the Saturday afternoon of August 24. Typical of the districts which took a heavy toll was the area around Green Road, Southsea, ***(above)*** *and also in Stanley Street, Southsea* ***(below).***

Eight people were killed when a bomb pierced the roof of the Princes Theatre in Lake Road on August 24, 1940, demolishing the building, but there were lucky escapes for the rest of the audience, made up largely of children.

HANDLEYS

WILL DEFINITELY

RE-OPEN

TO-MORROW

(Wednesday)

All departments, including
Cafe - - Orchestra as usual

☆ *There are air raid shelters for customers in addition to our staff shelters.*

Customers who have placed their Furs in our care may rest assured that they are perfectly safe.

Shop wisely and with confidence at

HANDLEYS Ltd., SOUTHSEA

This defiant advertisement from one of Southsea's leading stores appeared only three days after the devastating air raid of August 24, 1940.

One minute they were homes, outwardly similar but every one stamped with the individuality of its owner. The next, these properties in Shearer Road, Buckland, were reduced to an anonymous pile of rubble by the bombers.

This huge crater on the Highbury Estate at Cosham ***(above)*** *clearly shows the destructive force contained in just one bomb. Thousands fell on Portsmouth and the towns around it, such as the blast* ***(below)*** *in Spring Garden Lane, Gosport.*

A narrow escape for the lovely old Bedhampton Manor ***(above),*** *its usually immaculate grounds disturbed by a sizeable bomb crater. Other areas also took a battering, such as Colenso Road, Fareham,* ***(below, left)*** *and Privett Road, Gosport,* ***(below, right).***

The Luftwaffe met fierce resistance from the Solent area's heavy anti-aircraft batteries. This Heinkel 111 came to grief at Denmead in July, 1940, and its crew were captured by two civilians, one of them a local publican "armed" with a toy pistol ***(below).*** *People flocked to his pub from miles around to see the plane and hear the story, and he almost sold out of beer in one evening.*

*The three-man crew of this Junkers 88 **(above)** were killed when it crashed near Woodberry Lane, Rowlands Castle, during the August 12 air raid. A sister plane **(below)** came to grief in a field at Southbourne.*

Blast had strange effects. While this house at Havant escaped with scarcely a crack in its brickwork, the roof was stripped of its tiles and every window broken.

More peculiar blast effects — in Edinburgh Road, Portsmouth, the fronts of these houses ***(above)*** *were sucked out, but in the home of the elderly resident peering out into the street, flowers stayed in their vase and a picture remained on the wall. The usual problem for public houses was a shortage of beer, with some of them opening their doors for only two hours a day. This time, instead of "Sorry, no beer", the sign* ***(below)*** *indicated plenty of supplies but no way of serving them.*

The night before Christmas Eve, 1940, a massive explosion shook the closely-packed area of Conway Street, Landport. Thirteen people were killed, scores injured, and hundreds made homeless as the year which had opened in an eerie quiet came to a shattering end.

The Navy's here — and the Army as well. Living in a major naval port may have meant that you were always on the enemy's target list but also ensured a ready supply of manpower to help out when things got tough. The ratings ***(above)*** *are seen clearing up in St James Road, Southsea, and the troops* ***(below)*** *are busy on salvage work at St Mary's Hospital.*

The Co-operative Store in Fratton Road ***(above)*** *was one of many major stores which fell victim to the fire blitz of January, 1941. In Commercial Road, Woolworth's, C. and A., the Landport Drapery Bazaar, and Timothy Whites all suffered, and at Southsea, Handley's and Knight and Lee's were badly bombed as well as shops in Kings Road.*

Once it was the city's premier shopping centre. Now Commercial Road is in ruins, with the burned-out shell of the C and A building on the right, the wreckage of the Landport Drapery Bazaar next to it, and the remains of the Royal Sailors' Rest in the background.

Unharmed amid the wreckage, the Cathedral ***(above)*** *towers over the ruins of Oyster Street in Old Portsmouth. Despite the fact that it was hit three times, the Royal Hospital* ***(below)*** *managed to evacuate all its patients safely, although several staff and a special constable were killed in the casualty department.*

The start of the end for Portsmouth's original Guildhall as fire breaks out in the roof on the night of January 10, 1941. It burned for more than 12 hours, and salvage workers had to wait days before the gutted interior ***(below, left)*** *was cool enough to enter. A few hundred yards away in Guildhall Walk, the Hippodrome* ***(below, right)*** *suffered a similar blow. Not long after this photograph was taken, it became another of Portsmouth's demolition sites.*

*The corner of Hyde Park Road and Russell Street **(above)**, where another shopping centre was wiped out. Twisted girders are all that remains of the once proud Handley's Corner at Southsea **(below)**.*

Kings had worshipped there, Charles II was married there, but the Royal Garrison Church's 700-year history almost came to an end in the fire blitz. Its shell is still preserved near the seafront at Old Portsmouth.

P.C. Goronwy Wynne Evans, the only member of the Portsmouth City police force to be awarded the George Medal during the war. He won it tackling a fire in Elm Grove, Southsea, during the air raids of March, 1941.

Time for a cuppa ***(above)*** *at one of the street refreshment centres which were hastily set up after the raids. This one is outside the ruined Guildhall.* ***Below,*** *in typically pugnacious pose, Prime Minister Winston Churchill tours Portsmouth after the January, 1941, blitz. With him (right) is Mr. Harry Hopkins, President Roosevelt's special envoy, and behind them is the Regional Commissioner, Mr. Harold Butler. On the left is Admiral Sir William James, at that time Commander-in-Chief, Portsmouth, but later in the war to become one of the city's M.P.s.*

Large areas of the city were in ruins, but the visit of the King and Queen in February, 1941, put smiles back on the people's faces. Enthusiastic crowds greeted them throughout their tour, and they frequently broke off to talk to residents, salvage workers, and men from the forces. With them **(below)** *in the background is the Town Clerk, Mr. Frederick Sparks, who was also the city's A.R.P. Controller and was knighted a short time afterwards.*

Making sure that they saw as much as possible during their brief visit, the King and Queen found time to talk to Servicemen and civilians alike.

Its turrets defiantly standing, St Paul's Church at Southsea is otherwise a ruin. Known as the Mother of Southsea churches, it was built in 1822 and was said to possess one of the widest roof spans in the South of England.

Floors lean drunkenly as salvage work begins in The Strand at Southsea, one of the areas hit during the raids of March, 1941.

A landmark in the city for many years, the towering Central Hotel in Commercial Road had to be demolished in 1942 after being burned out and made unsafe during the 1941 blitz. Note the two men busy with pickaxe on the top parapet of the building.

Hayling came in for extra punishment during the fierce raids in April, 1941, when an entire anti-aircraft battery there was destroyed. ***Above,*** *the scene of devastation at West Town and* ***(below),*** *the hole made by a time bomb.*

And still the raiders came. ***Above,*** *residents of Bramshott Road, Southsea, examine the damage after one of the April raids, and* ***(below),*** *more of those made homeless by the bombs in the spring of 1941 prepare to leave the city.*

Ready for action. Men of an anti-aircraft battery ***(above)*** *prepare to give the enemy bombers a hot reception in 1940. When the battle-hardened gunners went overseas in 1942, their places were taken by the new mixed batteries, with A.T.S. girls working range-finders and tracking the bombers.*

Above: *A call to action at the battery site at Hayling Island, destroyed by direct hits in April, 1941, with heavy loss of life.* ***Below, left:*** *A hot night-time reception for the enemy, and* ***(below, right)*** *a lone raider is caught by the camera as well as the gun sights over the Isle of Wight in 1940.*

Above: *Men of Southsea Common's anti-aircraft battery in cheerful mood in the sunshine of September, 1939.* ***Below,*** *A.T.S. women gather round for the post call at North Hayling's anti-aircraft site in March, 1943.*

*More family homes disappear from the map, this time in Kirby Road, North End, **(above)** in the summer of 1943. **Below:** This desolate scene at Hyde Park Corner, Southsea, was pictured in early 1942.*

Clearing up work starts on what was once a pleasant family home in Chichester. There was an additional tragedy for the city in May, 1944, when a crippled American bomber crashed near a housing estate, killing a young girl and damaging 200 properties.

***Above:** Not a junk yard but the aftermath of a bombing raid on Chichester. **Below:** A quiet residential street becomes a scene of devastation — the scene at Portchester at the end of April, 1944.*

*There was an enthusiastic reception for General Bernard Montgomery when he dropped in on Portsmouth in January, 1944, to revisit the city where he was garrison commander for two years before the war. The people did not know it, but it was a prelude to the biggest invasion in history. Ready for D-Day **(below)**, vehicles are loaded on to landing craft at Hardway, Gosport.*

*A formidable mass of material and men built up in Hampshire in the months before D-Day. This convoy **(above)** is pictured waiting in Mumby Road, Gosport, to embark in Beach Street as part of the Allied invasion force which left Portsmouth on June 6, 1944. Security was the watchword that summer, and **(below)** identity cards are carefully scrutinised at a railway station.*

The Germans' last fling at Portsmouth took the form of flying bomb raids in the final June of the war. Locksway Road at Milton was hit ***(above),*** *and the last bomb to fall on the city caused 15 deaths and scores of injuries in Newcomen Road, Stamshaw* ***(below).***

The Civilian Army

Dad's Army, they were affectionately called in later years. The men of the Home Guard, many of them serving when still in their seventies, were an essential part of the Home Front in the days when nothing seemed to stand between England and a German invasion.

They began life as the Local Defence Volunteers, parading in suits and sports jackets, using broomsticks to simulate rifles, their platoons including enthusiastic youths who were too young to join up, as well as a stiffening of old soldiers from the Kaiser's War.

That was in May, 1940, when most people were wondering not whether the Germans would invade, but how soon. Portsmouth may have been the country's premier naval port, but its desperate situation typified the nation's plight. The Guildhall's defences were revealed a few months after the war by Sir Denis Daley, who had been Lord Mayor at the time. "We got 48 sailors with 30 rifles — they were all the rifles in the city. We had some hand grenades and a machine gun, which was a worn-out Hotchkiss with a part missing. An armourer in the Dockyard made that part and it was hoped it would work." Fortunately, the gun was never put to the test and the civilian army had time to gather strength. In August, 1940, they were renamed the Home Guard, and as units sprang up throughout the country and uniforms and rifles began to trickle through, they became a familiar sight. Officially part of the forces of the Crown, they were subject to military law and by 1944 were more than two million strong.

Behind the initially makeshift army was a deadly earnestness, typified by the South Coast's determination to "stand by to repel boarders." There were huge national anti-invasion exercises such as the one in August, 1941, involving one million men. They took their training seriously, and indeed, several died during it. When Chichester Home Guard took part in a local exercise using live ammunition in 1942, four of them were wounded, one seriously.

Gradually, Britain's part-time army slipped into place among the other services and began to play its full part in the war. By the time local contingents stood down at the end of 1944, they had become familiar figures on guard duty, on training grounds, in the streets, and at anti-aircraft sites. They had their moments of glory, too. Members of one Home Counties company had a red letter day in the summer of 1941 when they captured a German spy, complete with radio transmitter and parachute. He was later shot in the Tower of London, the first execution there for more than 150 years.

Others won local fame for very different reasons, such as the elderly Home Guard who almost shot Portsmouth's Lord Mayor during the invasion scare of 1940. Describing the incident to an audience of veteran Servicemen two years later, Councillor Sir Denis Daley — himself a former Royal Marine — recalled: "I had to arrange for the defence of the Guildhall. France had collapsed and we did not know what was likely to happen. One old fellow — I don't know how old he was — had never seen a magazine rifle in his life, but we served him and others with rifles. They were all grand fellows and they were stationed in the Guildhall. They had passed the stage when they could effectively use the butt of a rifle, so we served them with ammunition. They formed up inside the Guildhall on the ground floor and we gave the order to load. They loaded and closed the bolts. Then the old fellow wanted to see how it worked. He pressed the trigger and a shot whizzed past my ear."

There were other incidents which found an echo in a highly popular television series 40 years later. At Waterlooville, a Home Guard officer — a bank manager — was fined for showing a light during a blackout. The warden who reported him had apparently earlier been dismissed from the officer's platoon. In Chichester, magistrates decided that "not even a member of the Home Guard can be excused the use of foul language to the police when the latter are carrying out their duties." The case arose because a Home Guard man was stopped for cycling without lights. As the Battle of Britain was at its height at the time, and as he may have had other things on his mind, his reply to the zealous constable can well be imagined. Nevertheless he was fined £1 10s, double the usual amount.

That fateful battle obviously made some Home Guard volunteers a little too keen, and in August, 1940, Major Sir Jocelyn Lucas, the M.P. for Portsmouth South, was prompted to raise the matter in the House of Commons. He asked the Air Minister whether he would consider offering a £5 reward to anyone who captured an enemy parachutist alive, "thereby minimising the risk now taken by our own as well as enemy airmen shot down or escaping by parachute, since at present they are sometimes in danger of being shot in mid-air by over-zealous marksmen, despite all orders to the contrary."

Nor was age any barrier to enthusiasm. Typical of the spirit of the "old brigade" was Lieutenant H.J. Grant, who was 74 when he retired from the 17th (Portsmouth) Battalion in 1942. He and his platoon had twice been commended for the efficient way they carried out their duties during a general alarm and in the first blitz on the city, when they extinguished seven fires in their district. Elderly or not, there was no lack of volunteers and by the autumn of 1941 Portsmouth was ready to form its own Home Guard Cadet Corps for boys from 12 to 17 years old. They were not armed, and received no weapons training until they were 17. The accent was on first aid, scouting, signalling, gas drill, and physical training, and by October 24 that year, there had been 400 applications for the junior section (12 to 14) and 126 for the seniors (14 to 17).

There was plenty of scope for keen young men and in June, 1942, a Portsmouth contingent, led by a 19-year-old sergeant from North End, were claiming to be the first Home Guard section in the country to bring down an enemy plane. On their first night of duty after being transferred from infantry to anti-aircraft work, they helped to put up a heavy barrage during a German attack. The young sergeant, Frank Pascoe, said at the time that he had good reason for wanting to hit back as his own home had been destroyed by bombs and his best friend's family killed.

He was not alone in his feelings. Of the 70,000 properties in Portsmouth at the time, it was officially estimated that 65,000 were damaged during the war, some of them three or even four times. As entire streets disappeared under the German bombs, it posed an awesome task for the various authorities who were struggling to keep the city going during its ordeal by fire.

George Langrish, a member of the Auxiliary Fire Service at the time, can remember long, weary nights spent pumping water from Haslar Creek to the mainland while exploding bombs sent huge fountains of water into the air. At his home in Purbrook, he recalled: "Many's the time I looked at those water-spouts and thought about the amount of damage that stretch of water must have prevented and the number of bombs it must have absorbed." They were nights when the men snatched what sleep they could in vans, lorries, or sheds, and when they never knew whether they would be going home or be sent on somewhere else.

Based at Waterlooville, he and his colleagues were drafted wherever the need was greatest. "Pumps were being sent in all directions, water mains were being broken by bombs, and it was becoming more and more difficult to get a water supply, except from areas near the sea. Just after the Portsmouth blitz, we were sent to Southampton and I was a pump operator outside Edwin Jones's store. A bomb hit the water main, so I switched my pump to the bomb crater. It was a right old mixture that came out the other end, I can assure you."

Water was always the greatest need, and a post-war report by Portsmouth Water Company revealed just how critical the situation had become at one point. During the great fire blitz, about 60 mains were broken and many areas of the city were without water for five days. Daily consumption rose from 15 million to 23 million gallons, and the company's pumping plant was hard pressed to keep reservoirs from being completely emptied. To help overcome the shortage, about 30 miles of 12-inch surface water pipes were laid throughout the Portsmouth Garrison Command area to supply water from the sea. It was later estimated that these were capable of delivering about two million gallons an hour. Nearly 1,000 large static tanks were also set up in towns throughout the area, capable of holding another 20 million gallons between them. These brought their own problems, becoming a fatal attraction to several young children and also making ideal sites for dumping rubbish under cover of the blackout. When two at Southsea were drained for their periodical clean-up, nine tons of assorted junk were found in one and 11 tons in the other.

At the beginning of the war, the newly-formed A.F.S. had little equipment. Portsmouth's firefighters were part of the joint Police Fire Brigade, but the surrounding areas still relied on part-time retained firemen. Heavy private cars such as Armstrong Siddeleys were initially used for towing their equipment around, but gradually new equipment started to arrive, and by the time the National Fire Service was set up in the autumn of 1941, the South's firemen, already bloodied by two of the war's heaviest raids, were ready for anything. Indeed, formation of the N.F.S. was believed to have been directly due to Portsmouth's experiences during the blitz. With the city in flames, the Dockyard brigade had gone to help their fellow firemen, only to discover that their hose connections differed by a quarter of an inch and were therefore useless. Machines from London had also been sent, but it was discovered that their hoses clipped on to hydrants while Portsmouth's screwed on. All of this equipment became standardised after the formation of the N.F.S. In the autumn of 1942, the first contingent of Canadian fire-fighters arrived in the city, drawn from brigades throughout their native land. The 100 officers and men were to stay here for two years, giving particularly valuable assistance during the 1943 air raids.

While firemen worked tirelessly to salvage what they could from a city under siege, others were standing by to begin the painstaking task of extricating trapped or injured people from the rubble of their homes. During an air raid, news of trapped casualties would reach the rescue depot from wardens via a service control point, and a team would be dispatched immediately. Frequently a digging, shoring or tunnelling job would be carried on while men of the A.F.S. worked alongside, playing their hoses on the flames. The Rescue Service was a branch of the A.R.P. under the direction of the City Engineer. Each district had its own depot commanded by a superintendent, who was assisted by a number of women telephonists as well as party leaders and their deputies. Each party leader had seven men, including a lorry driver, skilled tradesmen from the building industry, and labourers, who were equipped with a truck and a trailer carrying ladders, ropes, tools, and stretchers. During the breathing space between raids, the Rescue Service was responsible for salvaging food, clothing, furniture and other possessions from bombed premises, as well as shoring or demolishing dangerous buildings.

As a reporter wrote in 1942: "If after a blitz you happen to be out early, and in the grey light of dawn you chance to see a forlorn little group of weary, dirty rescue men working away at a bombed house, probably gasping for a cup of tea from a mobile canteen they seldom see, you will know this: here are men (most of them formerly in reserved occupations) who volunteered to serve their country, offering themselves and their skill in order to perform that which is perhaps the most dangerous, arduous and necessary job of all — the rescue of trapped people in bombed houses; the saving of life; the job at which several men of the Portsmouth Rescue Service have made the supreme sacrifice."

There were heroic acts almost every day. Typical was 21-year-old William Lane, of Childs Square, Stamshaw, who was prevented by tuberculosis from joining the Army and became the leader of a first aid party. When a time bomb trapped two people in rubble in Kent Street, he and two colleagues, Albert White and Leonard Wilson, tunnelled their way through three brick walls in a confined space, using only a hammer and two axes, while bombs dropped around them and one lay unexploded only 30 feet away. After three hours, they reached the casualties, an exploit for which all three were awarded the George Medal.

Volunteers in the first aid posts could sometimes outrival the Home Guard as far as age was concerned.

When Surgeon Rear-Admiral Sir George Welch was advised to step down in 1943 as medical officer in charge of the post at Stone Lane, Gosport, he was not happy about it. Even at 85, he was still willing to soldier on if required, he said. Then there were men like Special Constable Edward Mansfield, of Eastney, an Indian Army veteran who had been commissioned in France during the first world war and was 74 when he finally stepped down from police duties in 1944. The "specials", War Reserve Constables, and Women's Police Auxiliary provided valuable assistance for the hard-pressed city force, even though their numbers had been drastically reduced from the pre-war figure. Formed in 1936, the Special Constabulary numbered 1,329 men by the time of the Munich crisis two years later. On the outbreak of war, call-up and evacuation reduced this figure to 815, and by the end of 1941 it was down to 462.

These were the men and women who dealt with the aftermath of the bombing raids. Thousands of others were engaged in trying to prevent the worst, either on fire-watching duties or as A.R.P. wardens. Compulsory enrolment for Civil Defence in Portsmouth was introduced for men aged between 18 and 60 on July 30, 1941. It was estimated at this stage that two million men and women were already undertaking Fireguard duties throughout the country, but the aim was to boost their number. To this end, the Fireguard service was strengthened into a national system approximating to the wardens' organisation, with paid officers and non-commissioned officers appointed.

Hampshire's Civil Defence personnel were tested during a county-wide exercise in the autumn of 1941, joined by the military, Home Guard, and regular and war reserve police. Portsmouth and Bournemouth were supposed to have suffered heavy casualties, Gosport was subjected to a theoretical attack, Fareham was assumed to be thrown into chaos with road and rail services out of action, and Havant was the target of a mock invasion. For the most part, the authorities declared themselves satisfied with the outcome, although deficiencies were brought to light. Gosport's A.R.P. Officer reported a lack of badly-needed messengers, and at Petersfield, Home Guards and police stopped a bus in which only two of the 35 passengers were carrying their gas masks.

Portsmouth's home defence "army" reached a peak figure of 5,400 during the preparations for D-Day, when it was widely expected that the Allied invasion would unleash a furious enemy bombing reprisal. By the end of that year, with the Allies well advanced into France and the threat from Germany receding, half of the Civil Defence organisation was stood down, and there was a reduction of a further 25 per cent in the spring of 1945. The war machine was winding down.

At least they had one rifle. Gosport's Local Defence Volunteers, as the forerunners of the Home Guard were known, parade for Colonel R.F.A. Sloane-Stanley, their commanding officer, in July, 1940.

By August, 1940, the name had been changed to Home Guard and gradually, uniforms were beginning to come through. Men of the Cosham unit are pictured here trying their boots for size.

Now in full kit, and better equipped with weaponry, Wickham Home Guard are seen preparing for action in the high summer of 1940, when the German invasion scare was at its height.

***Above:** Ready for action, men of Wickham Home Guard take aim — three of them directly at the camera — in the high summer of 1940. **Below:** Keeping a watchful eye on the ground and the air, Havant Home Guard take up positions in August, 1940, when dogfights dotted the sky as the Battle of Britain was fought out overhead.*

Fix bayonets! This Portsmouth platoon goes through the drill just before Christmas, 1940.

Do-it-yourself with a vengeance. Men of Gosport Home Guard decided to make their own armoured car on an old van chassis.

Men of the Dockyard 18th Battalion Home Guard take a breather during a commando course at Farlington in 1942.

*There were moments of relaxation, too, such as the smoking concert **(above)** which appears to be going with a considerable swing. **Right:** A contemporary cartoonist's view of Britain's part-time army.*

Cosham's Home Guard take time out for "char and a wad" while on exercises at Butser in February, 1944.

National Fire Service motor-cyclists undergo training in November, 1942. Note the special blackout fitments on the headlamps for diffusing light.

A test for the air raid siren in Commercial Road. On the left is Supt. A.E. Johnson, head of the fire service in Portsmouth for the early war years, and with him is Commander H.G. Badger, D.S.C., who was the city's A.R.P. Officer from the outbreak of war until mid-1941. After arranging many exercises which were adopted nationally for training purposes, and supervising A.R.P. work throughout the heavy 1941 raids, he retired on doctor's orders. He died in a naval hospital on June 30, 1942.

Well protected by sandbags, Auxiliary Fire Service men at Fareham try out their portable telephone.

Keeping watch — a member of the A.F.S. at Fareham.

The testing time was yet to come. Meanwhile, with accordion, mouth organ, ukulele, and saucepan lid cymbals, men of the Auxiliary Fire Service celebrate the first Christmas of the war at one of their depots.

Time for a fry-up in an A.F.S. billet in Portsmouth in October, 1939.

A portable water tank is put through its paces in the first month of the war. Shortage of water became a major problem during the heavy air raids of 1941, and led to the construction of miles of surface pipes as well as hundreds of static tanks.

A typical A.F.S. squad at the outbreak of war, two years before the National Fire Service was formed as a result of the fire raids on Portsmouth.

Although the main threat of a German invasion had passed by the winter of 1940, there was no relaxation in military precautions. Road signs had been removed in the second year of the war, and did not reappear until the spring of 1944. A typical anti-invasion exercise ***(above and below)*** *took place in October, 1941, involving regular troops, the Home Guard, and the police, with road blocks and traffic checks throughout the area.*

*Ready for the worst. A Royal Navy party takes up its anti-invasion post in a Portsmouth street in March, 1942 (above) and an armoured car keeps a lonely vigil on Portsdown Hill the following month **(below).***

*Men of the Royal Observer Corps **(above)** at their post in the spring of 1940. Their enthusiasm was not matched by the antiquity of their equipment. Almost as archaic were these sound locators **(below)**, intended to detect and track enemy aircraft, but in the event frequently unreliable.*

Members of the Regional Mobile Rescue Column take part in a realistic exercise to improve their efficiency under all sorts of conditions. The preparations were as well, for their skill was put to the test time after time.

Men of the Regional Mobile Rescue Column at one of their training centres.

A typical rescue and demolition squad, this one was based at the Anglesey Road council depot in Portsmouth and is pictured in September, 1939. Each group was equipped with its own trailer carrying ladders, ropes, tools and stretchers.

Rescue workers at training camp at Basingstoke in May, 1943.

A rescue squad practises at Cosham just weeks after war broke out.

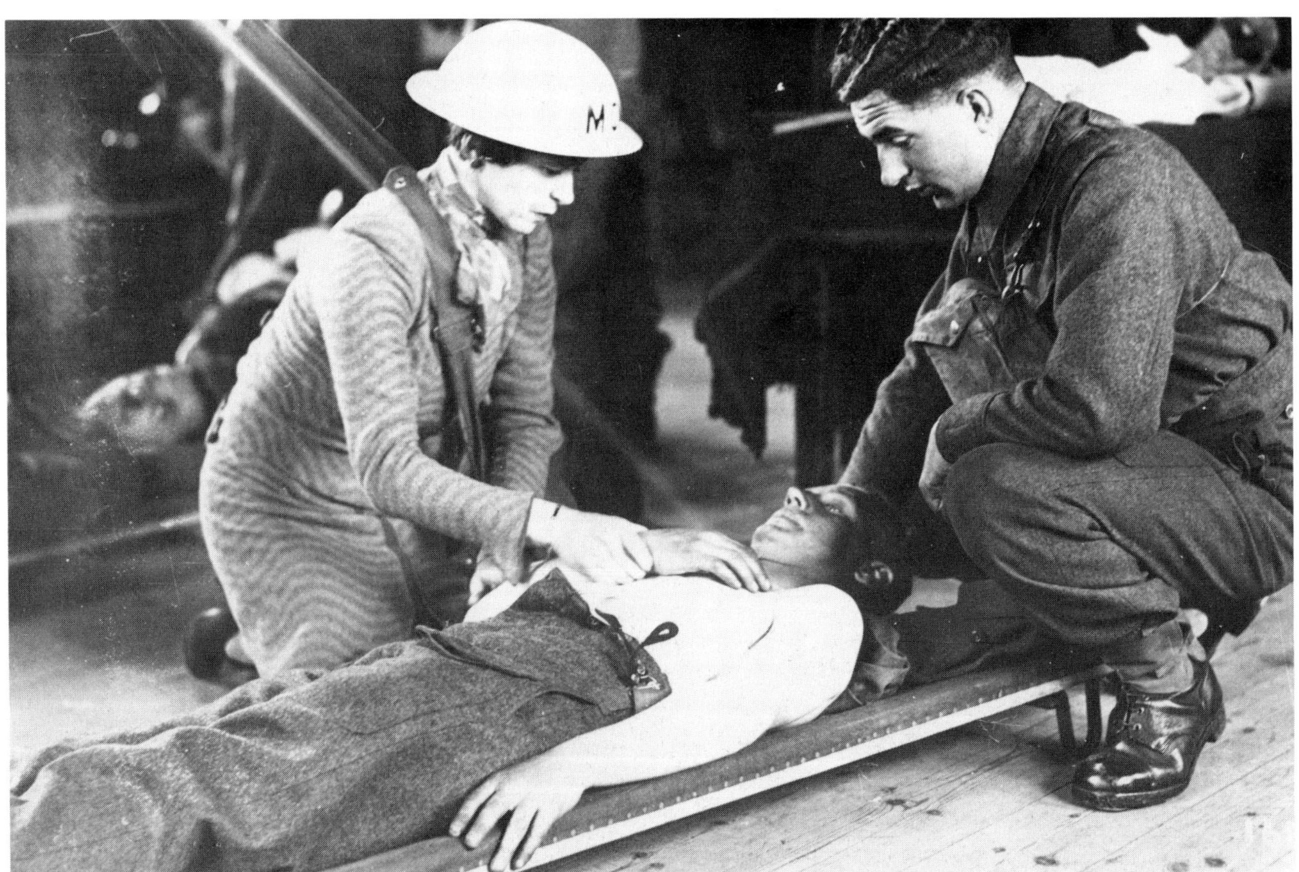

Dr. Una Mulvaney, medical officer in charge of a first aid post in St George's Square, Portsea, became a celebrated figure for her dedication to patients during the severest raids, and was made M.B.E. by the King for her work.

A group of volunteer ambulance drivers at Fareham early in 1940.

Even with wartime shortages, this Portsmouth first aid post managed to rustle up a brave display for harvest festival, including some precious bananas.

Every effort was made to see that life went on as normally as possible. An archway of walking sticks, crutches, and bandaged devices greeted this couple from No. 9 Cosham first aid post after their wedding at St Philip's Church in October, 1939.

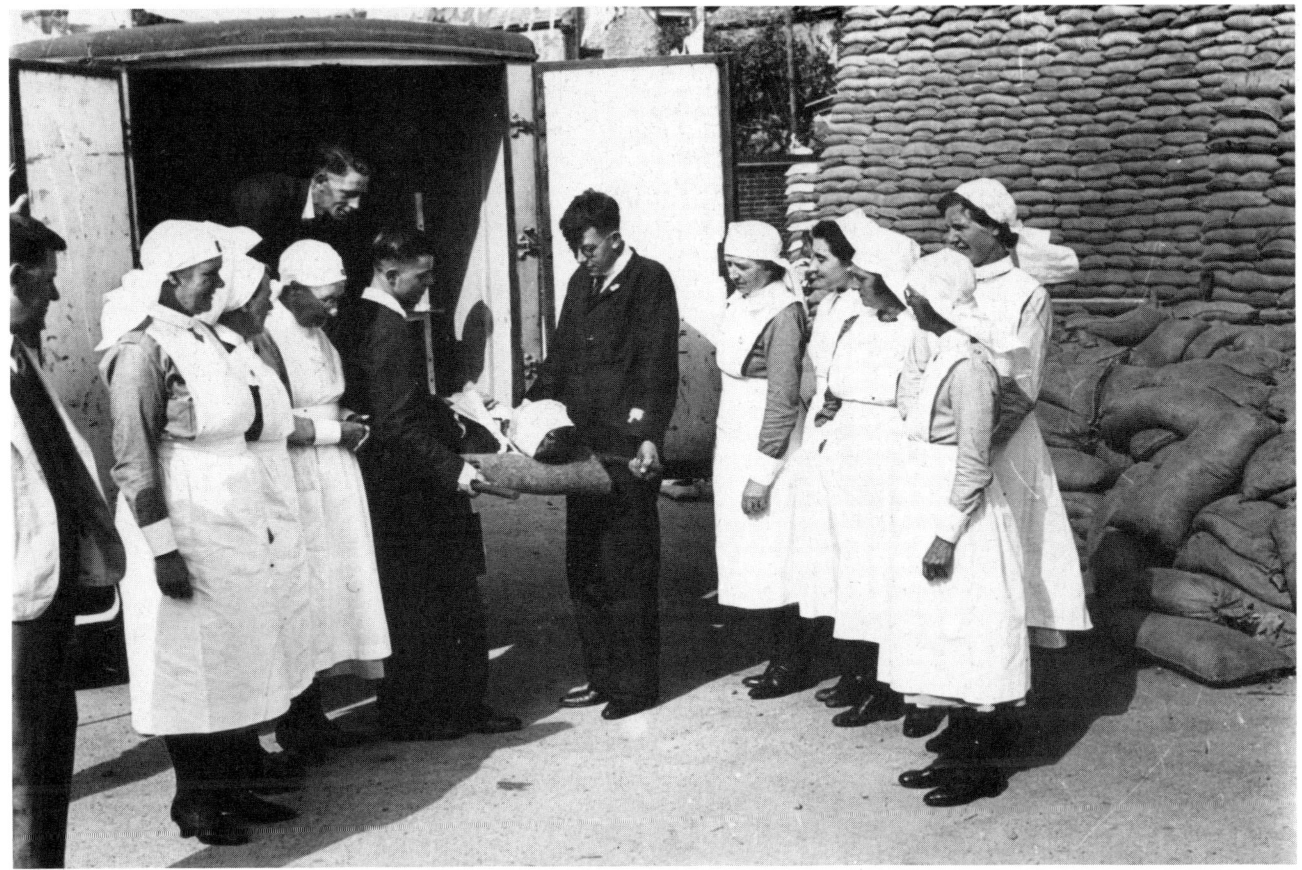

Volunteers get in some practice at Stone Lane first aid post, Gosport.

Brewing up at a mobile first aid post. The photograph was taken in October, 1939, when the nation was obsessed with the threat of chemical attack, which explains the anti-gas clothing worn by several personnel.

Nursing volunteers practise moving a casualty.

These A.R.P. wardens at Wymering were determined to put a brave face on things. Complete with dog mascot and Union Jack, they called their post "Young Bill's Better 'Ole", a reference to the celebrated first world war character Old Bill, and his slogan: "If you know of a better 'ole, go to it."

A wing-collared chairman supervises a conference of A.R.P. head wardens in February, 1940, when the efficiency of the blackout would doubtless have been high on the agenda.

There were few traffic jams in wartime, but everything stopped when the warden said so, as this drill in Copnor Road, Portsmouth, demonstrates in early 1940. Note the ambulance on the left with its bell on the running board.

Drivers and A.R.P. workers at Cosham with a vehicle typical of the sort which were presed into service as ambulances.

When salvage and rescue workers had done their bit after a raid, the men of the Pioneer Corps were called in to make safe any property. This photograph shows them about to demolish a dangerous wall in Green Road, Southsea.

Women at War

A woman's place was in the home — or at least, many people still thought it was in the autumn of 1939. But it did not take long for wives and mothers to become war workers just as a previous generation had done in 1914.

They drove ambulances and buses, staff cars and delivery vans. They manned mobile canteens in the dreadful bombing raids, joined up as Wrens, Waafs, A.T.S. and ack-ack girls, became nurses and police auxiliaries, and helped to cultivate the land in growing numbers. Those who could found part-time jobs to help the war effort, those who could not stayed at home and did their utmost to see that family life overcame the hunded and one restrictions and shortages of wartime.

Working habits changed, and factories rearranged shift patterns to fit in with women who could spare a few hours a day, but whose domestic ties prevented them working full-time. By the spring of 1944, Minister of Labour Ernest Bevin was able to report that of the country's 22 million who were fully employed or in the forces, more than seven million were women, a third of them married. "Cheerfully and willingly they have taken their part in the war effort at great inconvenience. Only a trifling few have had to be compulsorily directed to war work." They had worked long hours, sometimes up to 70 a week, and even in the fifth year of war, the average was 55.

It had not always been so. When the war started, the image of the "little woman" dominated by household routine and worries was still strong. You only had to look at newspaper advertisements of the day to see that the popular conception of a wife's main task in life was to keep her husbands shirts whiter than white. It had been all too easy to forget the immense contribution made by women in the previous war and to slip back into the old chauvinistic attitudes.

Propagandists reinforced that view in the early days. One potentially disastrous speech, intended for the Queen to broadcast but in the event dropped, was drafted by the celebrated children's writer A.A. Milne. It was intended as ammunition in the anti-gossip campaign, but even the Establishment obviously had second thoughts about the effect it would have had. Part of it ran: "You will have read for yourselves, and heard for yourselves, and perhaps had explained to you by husbands and fathers — who, as we women know, like explaining things to their families — just why we are at war today." It went on to refer to the blackout, and added: "It is you who have all the worry of the blinds and the curtains — whoever heard of a man bothering about such things? And food and rationing, that is our business again, isn't it? Women's work."

Women's work it may have been in the writer's eyes, but the people to whom it was almost addressed had other views. Had the speech ever gone out, it would have caused more than a few wry smiles in the railway workshops at Eastleigh, for example, where women clambered around huge steam locomotives, cleaning, greasing and repairing. At one stage, 700 of the 4,000 workers there were female, many of them putting in a 12-hour day as fitters, truck drivers, mechanics, and repairers. A reporter who toured the workshops wrote that "the hairstyles and make-up of the young girls are as immaculate as though they were doing a quiet office job. One efficient girl working a steam hammer in the blacksmith's shop was wearing a pair of fine silk stockings."

The railways were a temporary home to many others who found themselves employed as porters, at inquiry and ticket offices, at freight depots and warehouses, or driving lorries and vans on delivery rounds. In country districts, they were trained to assist signalmen, and others became waitresses on express trains, cooking and serving rationed meals to thousands of passengers each week.

London Transport employed thousands of women, mainly as conductresses on buses and trams, and they soon made their appearance in similar jobs throughout the country. Portsmouth had the distinction of providing the first women in England to take the wheel of a double-decker bus, Mrs E.V. Hunt and Mrs. K.E. Devine, who took to the road in 1941. By the end of that year, there were also 120 conductresses on the staff of the City Transport Department, filling jobs vacated by men who had left for the forces. They also appeared in the cabs of taxis, milk vans, post vans, bread vans, and coal delivery lorries. Hundreds more found jobs in Portsmouth Dockyard, and when the King visited the naval base in the autumn of 1942, he met many women workers at their benches.

At Havant, women were seen painting white lines in the middle of roads, and on the Hampshire-Sussex border, young enthusiasts of the Women's Timber Corps were busy felling beech trees to be used in building Mosquito aircraft. At Wickham, women formed work parties to sort, weigh, and pack an assortment of nuts, bolts, rivets and washers which had been swept up from the floors of aircraft factories, so that they could be used again. The scheme originated in the home of a W.V.S. clothing officer, spread to other parts of the country, and was the subject of a broadcast to America. Previously, factories had to take men or women away from their vital work to sort out urgently needed rivets and the like.

With the German U-boat blockade taking a terrible toll of Allied merchant shipping and imported food and materials, the need for self-sufficiency became paramount. "Dig for Victory" was one of the war's most famous slogans, aimed at encouraging householders to produce as much of their food as humanly possible.

While millions devoted their spare time to growing vegetables on every available spare inch of ground, others were following the exhortation to "lend a hand on the land". The Women's Land Army expanded by leaps and bounds until by the summer of 1941, there were more than 12,000 volunteers in regular employment, with new recruits coming forward at the rate of 500 a week. One group in Sussex worked through the coldest days of early spring helping to plough the South Downs. Others were busy hedging and ditching, or draining and clearing derelict land taken over by various committees. As one of them told the Duke of Norfolk at a huge rally at Arundel Castle in the summer of 1943: "We are conscious that there is not so much glamour about us as some of the Services, but let us say that if not glamorous, we are vital."

The Land Army found itself with a particularly sensitive matter to deal with in the autumn of 1943, when a coloured girl from East London was rejected for service. Officials said recruiting had ended and denied operating a colour bar, but questions were asked in the House of Commons and the matter threatened to escalate until a farmer at Wickham said he would take the girl provided the W.L.A. allowed her to become a member. Four villagers also came forward with offers of accommodation.

With more and more mothers being encouraged to join in the active war effort, an obvious problem was what to do with the children. One answer was the provision of day nurseries, and in June, 1942, Portsmouth's first opened at Kingston Cross, capable of accommodating 40 children under the age of five, and with its own air raid shelter and pram shed in the grounds.

Thousands of other women who found even part-time jobs impossible threw themselves into voluntary work, from providing canteen services for troops and rescue services to helping with relief work and raising money for aeroplanes. Typical of the organisations which co-ordinated their efforts was the Women's Voluntary Service, formed nine months before the outbreak of war. While some groups knitted articles of clothing for soldiers, sailors and airmen, others supplied hospitals and first aid posts with sterile dressings, and still more drove mobile canteens to all parts of the city as well as cocoa vans to air raid shelters.

One of their tasks in the summer of 1941 was to collect aluminium to go towards the manufacture of aircraft, and their efforts in Portsmouth resulted in the supply of more than eight and a half tons. A further 130 members were busy finishing camouflage nets for use on guns, tanks, lorries and tents. Mothers were also urged to send their daughters between the ages of 14 and 16 to help with the needleworking of naval jumpers and trouser suits.

The nation's increasing reliance on women war workers doubtless helped to prompt the formation of a Portsmouth branch of the National Married Women's Association in early 1944, when an enthusiastic audience packed Angerstein Hall to hear the national chairman declare: "Your status as wives and mothers is, legally speaking, that of serfs." Their aim, she explained, was for a financial partnership in which all money was equally divided after the housekeeping had been taken care of.

Others had more than housekeeping to think of at that time. One hundred feet underground at Fort Southwick, just outside Portsmouth, planning for the forthcoming Allied invasion of France was in full swing. The combined operations headquarters teemed with activity, staffed by a combination of Wrens, Waafs and A.T.S. personnel who were at the heart of one of the war's greatest secrets. The location of the headquarters was naturally closely guarded, and newspaper reports at the time said only that it was "near an English country town". For anyone entering, there were repeated challenges from sentries armed with automatic weapons, then a walk down 149 steps — there were no lifts — to enter the long, narrow tunnels from which branched the teleprinters, switchboards, coding rooms, plotting rooms, and offices which would handle the mass of signals passed to and from the beaches of Normandy. Women who were there at the time can still vividly recall the tension in the air on June 6, 1944, as they waited for the first radio messages to indicate that the landings had been made and D-Day was under way. And when those first voices crackled over the air from the northern coast of France, excitement everywhere mounted. There was still a long haul ahead, but at least it was the beginning of the end.

Little women, 1940 style. This was how one newspaper advertisement visualised the female role in the early days.

Members of the 6th Hampshire Company of the A.T.S. take a break at Hilsea College to catch up on the mail.

Cooks at the Southsea Common anti-aircraft battery work up a head of steam in the first month of the war.

These three sets of sisters were well on the way to making up their own A.T.S. platoon in Portsmouth. In the back row are Daphne, Angela and Zilla Whittle; middle row, Pamela, Juanita, and Daphne Terry Wood; and front row, Cicely, Joyce, and Daphne Bashford.

Wren drivers at the Royal Marines Barracks, Eastney, in September, 1939. Note the white stripes painted on their Morris Commercial truck, a common device to make vehicles stand out better in the blackout.

Wrens deep underground in the D-Day headquarters at Fort Southwick, where one of the most vivid memories for many was the climb up 149 steps to reach the outside world.

The underground room at Fort Southwick where hundreds of naval messages were decoded during the run-up to D-Day and the invasion itself.

All smiles from these members of the Women's Land Army, an organisation which admitted that it may not have carried the glamour of the Services, but was every bit as vital.

The harvest is in, and now this Women's Land Army volunteer gets ready for a spot of ploughing on Hambledon Down in October, 1939.

Stop me and buy one — latter-day milkmaids set off on their rounds at Bedhampton in the spring of 1940.

No worries about using up precious petrol on this milk round as a Women's Land Army member sets off from Bedhampton.

Members of the Women's Voluntary Service were kept busy at both ends of the needlework scale. ***Above,*** *they are pictured at Fareham knitting items for Servicemen, and* ***(below)*** *at Emsworth, proudly displaying the camouflage netting which they have just completed.*

Members of the Women's Auxiliary Air Force tether a barrage balloon in Portsmouth in April, 1942. Advertisements for balloon crews stipulated that women should be physically fit, have a minimum height of 5ft. 2in., and be aged between 17 and 43.

Watchful A.T.S. girls practise tracking enemy planes as part of the mixed anti-aircraft batteries which replaced all-male crews when the latter moved overseas in the middle war years.

Full steam ahead for these women ***(above and below, right)*** *who took on heavy jobs at the Southern Railway workshops at Eastleigh. At one stage, 700 of the 4,000 workers there were female, and their number included a mother of ten and a grandmother with six of her seven sons in the forces.* ***Below, left:*** *A typical poster urging women to play their full part in the war effort.*

Housewives wait their turn to try their hand at extinguishing flames with a stirrup pump, under the tuition of Servicemen.

Jam was something of a war-time luxury, but you could still make it yourself, as this group at Horndean is busy demonstrating in the autumn of 1941.

Tickets, please! A mixture of fashions for these temporary bus conductors, taking instruction on the old type of ticket punch from a regular employee. In Portsmouth alone, 120 women were employed in such jobs.

This house at Wickham was turned into a war "factory", where women volunteers gathered to sort out nuts and bolts swept up from aircraft factory floors, ready for use once again.

The first women in England to take the wheel of a double-decker bus were Mrs. E.V. Hunt and Mrs. K.E. Devine, both of Portsmouth.

Petrol may have been in short supply and rationed, but someone still had to operate the pumps.

These nurses called out to the wreck of a German bomber at Rowlands Castle in August, 1940, found there was no help they could give. The crew of three were killed instantly.

As the Battle of Britain took its toll of Britain's aircraft over the skies of southern England in the summer of 1940, the drive began to replace them and scrap metal became a valuable commodity. ***Above:*** *W.V.S. members with a harvest of aluminium at one of their collection points in Portsmouth.* ***Below:*** *this first aid post at Drayton was busy urging people to turn saucepans into Spitfires.*

The requisitioned ambulance in the background may have belonged to a mattress company, but there was no rest for this group of nurses, seen going through a keep fit routine to keep them on their toes.

A volunteer driver in a hastily-converted laundry van gets her instructions from Dr. L.H. Cope, Medical Officer, in the autumn of 1939.

Improvised ambulances gradually gave way to purpose-built vehicles as the war effort built up and supplies started to come through. Here, volunteer ambulance drivers at Fareham familiarise themselves with their gleaming new machine.

Women of the First Aid Nursing Yeomanry make a practice dash for their vehicles in October, 1940.

Well known as A.R.P. telephonists, these twin sisters pictured at their Portsea post with a colleague were Betty and Eileen Fortune, inevitably known as the Miss Fortunes. They were so alike that they wore different coloured blouses to help their friends avoid mistakes.

Three A.R.P. wardens demonstrate a special motorised fire pump, mounted on a converted wheelbarrow.

A welcome sight for all Servicemen and women was the arrival of the food van and a welcome break for refreshments. Mobile canteens were in use throughout the area for rescue workers, firemen, and policemen as well as troops.

Gas masks firmly in position, this group of A.T.S. recruits undergo fire-fighting training.

*In the build-up to D-Day, dispatch riders get their orders from an A.T.S. officer at the headquarters of Southern Command. The A.T.S. itself provided dispatch riders, such as the sergeant **(below)** pictured on her Royal Enfield motor-cycle.*

*Waafs at work **(above)** on a Beaufort of Coastal Command in the summer of 1943. The Women's Auxiliary Air Force was originally known as the Women's Royal Air Force, which it again became in 1949. **Below, left:** Vehicle maintenance was one of the tasks cheerfully undertaken by the women of the A.T.S. **Below, right:** Anyone for tennis? A corporal stops to chat with a colleague (note the anti-blast tape fixed to the inside of the windows, a familiar feature of houses during the war).*

Wrens service a Seafire, the naval version of the celebrated Spitfire, at the Royal Naval Air Station at Lee-on-Solent in May, 1943.

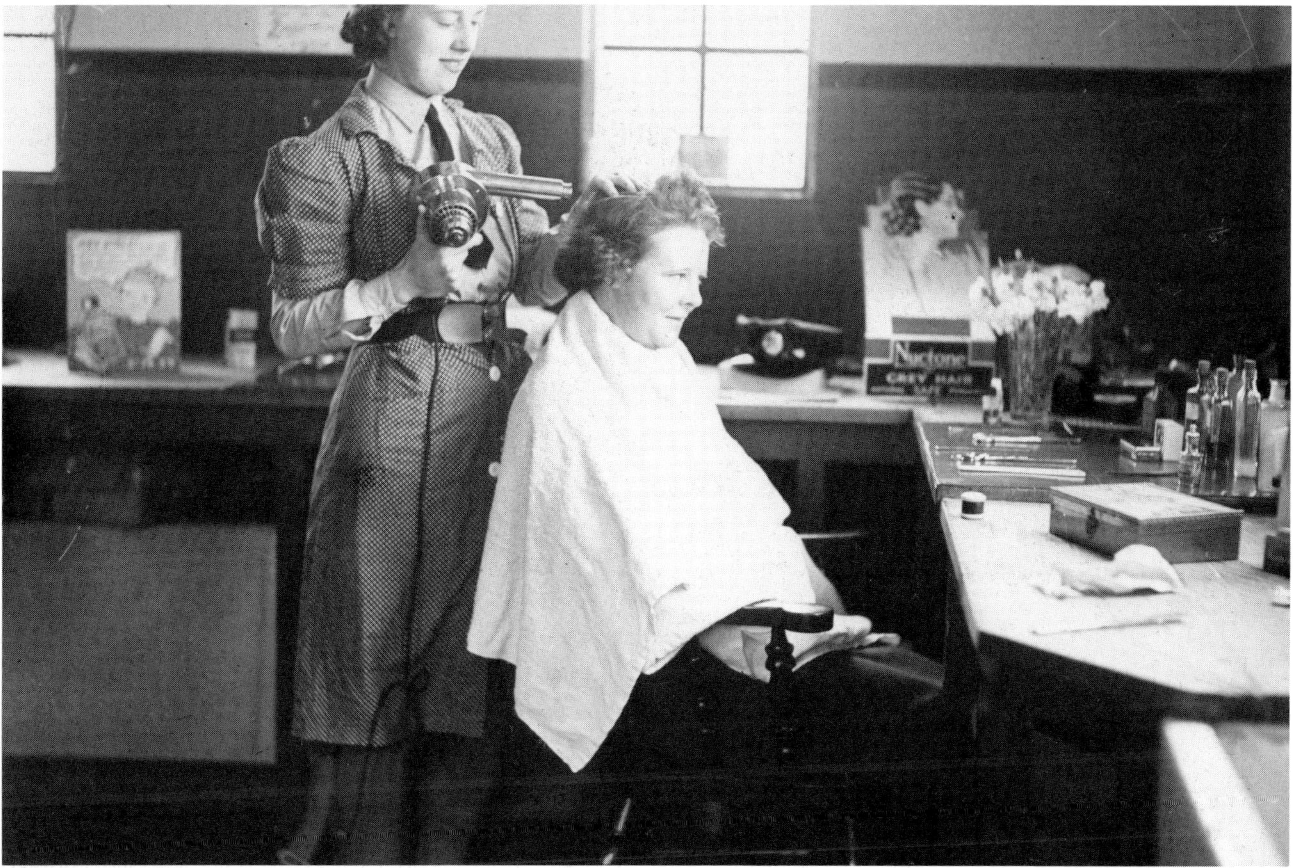

Waafs were busy on barrage balloon duties, such as the unit at Titchfield which celebrated its third anniversary in June, 1942. Here one of the crew gets a birthday hair-do for the occasion.

The only horsepower on this woman's milk round was provided by Shanks's pony.

These women ambulance volunteers in their special protective helmets are pictured at the Royal Portsmouth Hospital in September, 1939. Their job became increasingly important as the war went on, and by 1942, their fleet of vehicles had been augmented by two ambulances bought from the proceeds of selling millions of old copies of the Evening News as waste paper.

Major Sir Jocelyn Lucas, M.P. for Portsmouth South, meets a group of A.R.P. workers. He came up with several offbeat ideas during the war, including the suggestion in February, 1940, that in view of the close co-operation between the French and British armies, our cooks should have a course of instruction under French chefs.

Wrens on parade for their Controller, Dame Laughton Matthews, in the spring of 1945. The first Wrens had sailed for overseas service six months earlier. Signallers and writers, they had volunteered for duty on communications work in Normandy.

□More than 57,000 people had been killed in air raids on Britain, the Home Secretary, Mr. Herbert Morrison, announced in February, 1945.

□"There was one thing that Hitler left completely out of his calculations when he started on his mad course of world domination, and that was the voluntary spirit of Great Britain. The Nazi mind just could not grasp such an idea. The voluntary spirit, as exemplified by the Home Guard, has the admiration of the world."

Major-General H.D. Curtis, G.O.C. Aldershot and Hampshire District, on the disbanding of the Home Guard in Portsmouth in December, 1944.

□If you've news of our munitions, keep it dark
Ships or planes or troop positions, keep it dark
Lives are lost through conversation,
Here's a tip for the duration
When you've private information, keep it dark

War-time verse as part of the Government's anti-gossip campaign.

□A captured enemy plane was put to good use in Chichester in October, 1940, when a Messerschmitt which had crashed went on show in the central car park to raise money for the Hurricane Fund. Over the first weekend, nearly 2,000 people paid to have a closer look at it.

□The nightly quest for beer became a feature of wartime life as pubs frequently sold out long before the normal closing time. Some licensees resorted to secret arrangements for opening side doors to regular customers at prearranged times, while others complained about "poachers" who dodged around from pub to pub depriving the usual customers of their ration. Publicans explained away the greater demand for beer by the fact that the wartime brew was of far lower gravity than usual and had little "kick."

All smiles from this group of willing female workers at the Ranelagh Yacht Yard at Wootton, in the Isle of Wight, in February, 1945. They are holding a small assault boat, several thousand of which were built during the war.

Putting across a vital message — women from the Milton area of Portsmouth take their slogans into the streets after the city's second air raid in August, 1940.

Waafs and their officers join in a sing-song to celebrate the third anniversary of the formation of Titchfield Balloon Centre, in June, 1942.

□When the Landport Drapery Bazaar advertised that a consignment of rayon stockings was arriving at its shop in Kingston Road, Portsmouth, at the end of August, 1944, it caused such a queue that a photograph of the patiently waiting women appeared in the Evening News. Only 2,500 pairs were available, and each shopper was rationed to one pair.

□Summer holidays took on a different meaning for many people because of the wartime labour shortage. During their annual break, factory workers joined office workers in the fields at harvest time, picking fruit and vegetables at special holiday camps organised by the Ministry of Agriculture. They paid 28s (£1.40) a week for their accommodation, and in return received a shilling an hour (5p) for their efforts. The scheme proved so popular that by the summer of 1944, one Hampshire camp was booked up until the end of September.

□A bonus issue of bacon brightened the summer of 1944. For two months, the weekly allowance of four ounces per person was raised to six ounces.

□Binoculars for the armed forces were in great demand in the first year of the war — so much so that the Ministry of Supply advertised for members of the public to hand over their own, either for sale or as a gift. Opticians acted as collecting agents in every town, and 125,000 pairs were urgently sought in the winter of 1940.

Towards the Peace

The talk may have been almost entirely of the longed-for peace, but 1945 began as bleakly as any of the war years. For a start there were the continuing flying bomb attacks on southern England, which took a steady toll of civilian life. Then it was the coldest January for 50 years, with blocks of ice appearing in the harbour near Portsbridge, and the moat and Baffins Pond frozen hard. To add to the misery, coal supplies were in chaos and many homes were without fires. Merchants were up to a month behind in their deliveries as more and more staff fell sick because of the weather, others were drafted into the Army, and transport was defeated by snow and ice. Queues waited for hours in the hope of getting a few pounds of the precious fuel, but hundreds went home empty-handed. The situation became so serious that the coal dump on Southsea Common was opened to the public on condition that people collected their own supplies, which were limited to 28lb. each. Women with prams and pushchairs joined those who lined up for their ration, and in Southsea, coal was delivered by boys pulling sledges. There were the obvious complaints, but as one housewife stoically observed: "It's a lot worse in Berlin."

The year had begun hopefully enough. Indeed, Portsmouth's welcome to 1945 was the noisiest New Year celebration for six years. As the clock struck 12, locomotive whistles, factory sirens, church bells, motor horns and ships' hooters joined in a vast chorus that kept up for half an hour. At the city's cathedral, the bells rang out for the first time since 1938. According to the Evening News, "it left no doubt that 1944, a year of such momentous happenings at home and abroad, had departed giving place to another which it was hoped would bring peace and goodwill to all men throughout the civilized world." There was a special treat in store for nearly 500 children when American troops helped to put on a belated Christmas party in the civilian canteen at Hilsea. The young guests were given paper hats made out of battery and gum wrappers, as well as gifts of sweets, biscuits, and the prized candy bars which the men had saved from their rations.

But although peace may have been in sight, there was a long way to go before the sorely-tried people of the South could afford to relax. Villagers at Horndean were given a sharp reminder of this on the night of February 4, when an aircraft which had got into difficulties over Portsmouth crashed on top of Horndean Hill after first hitting a cottage in which four children were sleeping, then cutting the parish hall in two and ploughing into an embankment. The children had a miraculous escape and slept through the entire incident, despite a gaping hole over their bed. Wreckage was scattered high and wide, with parts of the plane falling into the local policeman's garden and other pieces near the War Memorial in the village centre. Luckily there were no civilian casualties, but the crash killed the plane's occupants, who were thought to have been trying to ditch in the sea to avoid a heavily populated area.

The hardships of war continued, but more and more people were turning their attention to the future and the new towns which would rise on the bomb sites. Planning was already well advanced. Even before the first Allied troops had set foot on the shores of northern France the previous summer, officials and councillors were busy looking at the shape of things to come. Their major preoccupation was obviously the rebuilding of the shattered areas and the rehousing of their bombed-out people and businesses. But apart from this, they knew that it would be a very different world. Six years of war had accelerated a host of developments, from building techniques to transport, and the post-war age would need to take account of them.

There was, for instance, the jet plane, which had sent people in the South of England diving for shelter when it made its first flight in late 1943, its whistling kettle sound convincing them that a huge bomb was on its way. By late 1944, Portsmouth was bidding for a "super air terminus" in Langstone Harbour, with three giant runways to cope with the new breed of aircraft which would make it among the finest in the world. This huge undertaking was intended to be home for flying boats as well as conventional passenger aircraft, and was a revival of the pre-war Empire air base scheme which had captured the area's imagination in 1933. Detailed plans were drawn up and countless meetings discussed the subject, but it never came to fruition.

Then there were dreams of new road links. One bold plan discussed by the city's Chamber of Commerce in the autumn of 1944 was for a motorway from Bognor to Portsmouth which would pass through Selsey and Wittering, crossing by bridges to Hayling and Portsmouth, and proceeding through a tunnel to Gosport.

But the major consideration was still housing, and the need to ensure that the citizens of the new Portsmouth had room to breathe. There had been too many houses crowded cheek by jowl in the old city, and the blitz, cruel though it was, did provide an opportunity to rebuild in a more spacious manner. This in turn meant that a large number of the 260,000 inhabitants would have to be rehoused outside the city boundaries, and plans were drawn up for a number of satellite towns. The biggest step in this respect was taken on February 8, 1944, when the City Council bought 1,700 acres of the Leigh Park estate as the site for one of its overspill areas. It cost £122,465, or about £75 an acre. There were to be other satellite towns at Purbrook and Crookhorn. Another huge chunk of land at Paulsgrove and Wymering, including the raceourse, was bought for

£105,000 early in 1945 as the site for "a self-contained suburb of the city" housing some 9,000 people. There were also plans to modernise Paulsgrove railway halt.

Strange new homes had already started to appear in other places, prefabricated buildings which could be erected much faster than conventional homes. Portsmouth was chosen as the trial area for the aptly-named Phoenix bungalows, and in February, 1945, bulldozers moved on to a site at Northern Parade in Hilsea to clear the way for more than 50 of them. Their erection started in May, and the first were opened six weeks later. At the Highbury Estate at Cosham, another new type of temporary house was being tried out, this time supplied by America under the Lend-Lease scheme. One hundred bungalows, made of wood and waterproof pulp board, started to go up at the end of the summer, and by mid-October, 80 of them had been completed. The need for new homes was so great that in December that year, the Health Committee decided that 260 three-bedroomed "prefabs" should be built without delay on the new Paulsgrove estate. While fresh homes went up, old ones came down. At Fratton Bridge, the last of several 300-year-old wooden cottages were demolished, although similar wooden habitations still existed at Ferrol Road in Gosport.

Another sort of wooden home caused an uproar shortly before Christmas, when it was revealed that a former first world war sergeant, his wife, their four sons — all ex-Royal Navy — and a daughter with a baby were living in a chicken shed at Wickham. Their plight was brought to the public's attention by the parish council which, tired of waiting for official action, told the family to take the law into their own hands and move into a nearby hut which had been used to house evacuees. The council added that if anyone in similar difficulties wished to move into the huts, "they will have our backing." There were others who found unorthodox remedies to the desperate housing shortage, including a mysterious group known as The Vigilantes, who operated throughout the country and encouraged what would today be known as squatters. One of their cases concerned a petty officer's wife with two children under the age of three, who was sharing a house at Fareham with two other families. Desperate for a place of her own and unable to get help from the council or other societies, she discovered a house in Bramble Road, Southsea, which had been empty for five years. She wrote to the nearest Vigilante group at Brighton, who told her: "Possession is nine points of the law. Go to it and best of luck." The woman moved in, told a reporter that she had the rent money ready if the owner arrived, and proceeded to clear away the dirt of the war years. By coincidence, the following day councils throughout the country received a circular from the Ministry of Health giving them powers to requisition empty houses without consulting anyone. Within a week, Portsmouth had requisitioned 68, but it was a mere drop in the ocean compared with the scale of the problem.

In the public sector, meanwhile, the planners had already unveiled a huge and remarkable model in April, 1944, showing their ideas for the centre of Portsmouth after the war. The rebuilt Guildhall, with a redesigned interior, faced a huge square and gardens in place of Greetham Street and the old railway goods yard, with administrative offices and other civic buildings on one side and blocks of flats on the other. By the beginning of 1945, there were firm plans for rebuilding the Southsea and North End shopping centres, plus industrial sites at Portsea and Fratton. The City Planning Officer (Mr. F.A.C. Maunder) told a conference of local politicians: "We have planned boldly, but we have not gone haywire."

While architects and builders conjured up their grand and sweeping schemes, the people of the area had more mundane matters on their minds. The Great Potato Debate was one. This broke out in the final April of the war, originally as a result of sudden shortages and huge queues, but built to a crescendo when the subject of German prisoners-of-war was introduced. The Government's official explanation for the lack of potatoes was bad weather, but one angry Eastney housewife demanded in a letter to the Evening News: "Why not tell people the truth and say we also have thousands of Germans to feed. All the women in the queues agree with me that the Germans should have potato peeling soup (and less), which they are giving to our men. We will gladly put out our peelings in the swill bucket to be collected for them." This letter was endorsed a few days later by a Fratton woman, who added: "The potato peeling soup she speaks of is almost too good for them. Give them what they gave our prisoners, and save decent food for decent English people to enjoy." A third "disgusted" correspondent drew attention to the recently published photographs of German torture chambers, "yet we feed the German prisoners like fighting cocks" and allow them to be "sunbathing and kept in luxury in the heart of this blitzed city." The intensity of feeling became so great that the matter was raised in the House of Commons by an Independent M.P. When one man wrote in to deplore "hate propaganda", and to point out that not every captured German soldier was a Nazi torturer, it provoked an avalanche of replies which fed the letters column with fresh fuel.

Gradually, though, the shortage abated, memory of the winter faded, and the South Coast settled down to enjoy one of the hottest Aprils for years. Civil Defence parties had been clearing beaches so that they could be reopened for the first summer season for five years, and even a cheerless and overcast Easter at the beginning of the month did not deter the crowds. They flocked to the piers and to Eastney to watch the Royal Marines Beat Retreat, cinemas and theatres were filled, the Leigh Park Hounds met on Stockheath Common, and "cyclists and ramblers streamed back into the city in the evening loaded with primroses and cherry blossom." Then the weather suddenly turned, and as the temperature rose into the upper seventies, thousands basked on the newly-opened seafront or queued up at the Canoe Lake, while crowds of youngsters bathed at Portsbridge. The mood everywhere was lighter. With the Allied armies at the gates of Berlin, it was obvious that the continuation of the war could now be counted in days, and when the total surrender of the Germans was announced on May 7, the pent-up emotion of the nation burst into open celebration. On the following day, officially declared as VE-Day, ships' sirens and hooters in Portsmouth Harbour screamed out a wild chorus of joy for half an hour. The Union Jack vied with the Stars and Stripes as a house decoration, bunting fluttered in the streets, and many girls either wore patriotic hair ribbons or entire outfits of red, white and blue. For once, housewives did not mind the queues when shops opened for a few hours, and for the first time in six years, the Dockyard was silent and closed with ships idle at their moorings. Gradually, crowds drifted towards the city's natural hub and gathered in their thousands in front of the burned-out Guildhall for a service of thanksgiving. At Cosham, effigies of Hitler were burned, while in towns and villages throughout the area, street parties, community singing, and dances were the order of the day.

As night fell, a huge crowd estimated at 25,000 filled Guildhall Square and stretched under the railway arch and along Russell Street into Greetham Street. The King's speech was broadcast from a police wireless unit, but nothing had been officially organised after that. The crowd needed no prompting to make its own entertainment. A variety of instruments appeared, singing and dancing began, and despite police precautions, some brave souls made their way into the Guildhall tower to start an impromptu bell ringing.

Bonfires had been officially banned, but when someone set fire to a newspaper near the junction of Commercial Road and Greetham Street, it was the signal for a victory conflagration. Other newspapers were thrown on, then the bases of flagpoles from Guildhall Square, and then the trestles which had been used to keep the crowds in position during that morning's thanksgiving service. The Corporation yard at the side of the station was raided for fresh supplies, and tools, air raid notice boards, and even the gates of the yard itself joined the growing pile, followed by seats from Victoria Park. It was all good-humoured enough, but police were worried that things might get out of control, and called a National Fire Service unit to damp down the flames. While the fire officer in charge was deciding that there was little damage from the bonfire, enthusiastic revellers were "liberating" his fire equipment to add to the dancing flames.

When another huge crowd gathered the following night, police and naval patrols were ready guarding anything combustible, but even so a second bonfire was started, and the huge indicator board in front of the Guildhall which had showed the progress of war savings throughout the war was smashed up and burned. Some householders had an unhappy reminder of the blitz when several shells containing parachute flares failed to explode in mid-air and damaged property on the Highbury Estate at Cosham. One fell through a roof in Hawthorn Crescent, narrowly missing a sleeping child, and another crashed into the bedroom of a house in Chatsworth Avenue.

This was nothing, however, compared with the explosion the following month which rocked whole areas of Surrey when an ammunition dump at a Canadian Army repatriation camp at Witley exploded with a roar which could be heard 20 miles away. It was like a horrible firework display, according to one eyewitness, but fortunately no one was killed and only four soldiers injured. Even so, for men waiting to return to their homeland, it was an unpleasant reminder of the war they had survived.

In Portsmouth, meanwhile, other men were waiting to go home — the first draft of naval and Royal Marines personnel to become eligible for demobilization. On June 18, the initial batch of 300 lined up at the Portsdown Motor Garage at Cosham, which had been turned into a giant store to issue civilian clothes in exchange for the uniforms they had worn for six years. They had already been through the dispersal centre at Stamshaw Camp, where paybooks and other Service papers had been brought up to date. Now they were ready to receive their final bounty from the Royal Navy, a complete issue of clothing which included everything from raincoat to collar studs and cufflinks. It was all planned to the last detail, and the centre's boast was that it could deal with 40 men an hour and kit out each member of the new civilian army in 15 minutes. A reporter who visited the centre on its first day wrote that "the sailor certainly gets a good first impression. The ratings who welcome him might well be experienced shop-walkers. They show him to a chair in front of a show window in which are displayed some of the styles of suits, shirts and collars. It is in a showpiece in a setting of primrose and green, and above it is written "Clothing of Distinction." The sailor waits his turn to be measured, and while waiting reads a magazine or listens to the wireless."

A civilian supervisor with 36 years' experience in the retail trade gave the fledgling civilians a final inspection, and anyone of what was tactfully described as an "awkward" size was assured that his suit would be ready in six weeks. As the officer in charge explained: "Sailors are very particular. They will have the right thing. Remember, they have to go home to their wives." Transport to the railway station was provided, and all those facing a journey of more than six hours were given a packed meal to take with them. One of the assistants added: "Up to now we have made everybody happy. They go out smiling." Others managed to keep smiling even though they had to wait for their demobilization. Fine weather had already brought crowds flocking to the beach at Southsea, and a few miles along the coast, Wrens from the camps at Stockheath and West Leigh soaked up the sun at Hayling, while sailors lined up for bathing parade to the music of a band which entertained them on the beach. Day trippers were out in their hundreds, and visitors found an unusual attraction in the Camber Dock at Portsmouth, where a captured German E-boat was put on show to the public.

There were no smiles, however, in the seemingly endless queues, where murmurs of protest were growing. With the war in Europe over for more than two months, voices were raised about the continued shortages. Portsmouth Women Citizens Association, weary of what they called a tax on their time and patience, wanted to know whether the eternal food queues were due to lack of supplies, shortage of labour, or bad allocation. The Evening News commented: "For months now, the sight of harrassed housewives standing in all weathers and at all times for anything from fish to fruit has long been a far too common one. The country has quietly borne the queue burden since 1940, but housewives consider that they are now entitled to a better deal." An official of the Ministry of War Transport replied: "It seems to have been overlooked that the manpower problem is still with us, and that much of the queueing is due to the fact that shopkeepers are now having to manage with one or two assistants, whereas before the war they employed four or five."

On the morning of July 5, housewives were out in force, not seeking groceries this time but following official advice to vote early in the country's first postwar general election and thus avoid one more queue. It took three weeks to count all the ballot papers from Servicemen and women around the world, and when the result was announced on July 26, a Labour landslide was revealed, with several national war-time figures being voted out of office. The Socialists gained two of Portsmouth's three seats, with Captain Julian Snow capturing Central and Major Donald Bruce taking North. Major Sir Jocelyn Lucas held Portsmouth South for the Conservatives, but with a vastly reduced majority.

Politics and even shortages took a temporary back seat at the end of that month, when holidaymakers arrived by the trainload in Portsmouth, 14,000 of them bound for the Isle of Wight. The three paddle steamers which were left to ferry them there struggled manfully throughout the day to clear the immense backlog which built up at the Harbour Station. At one stage an estimated 4,000 people were patiently waiting — in queues, naturally — for a ticket to Ryde, and the last passenger was not cleared until the 8.05 p.m. boat left. Four days later, on August Bank Holiday, crowds queued in ranks ten and 12 deep at Waterloo for the special excursion trains, many having spent the night resting on suitcases or collapsible stools. The demand for Southsea and the Isle of Wight was so great that special relief trains had to be put on, and cross-Solent boats were busier than ever. The holiday mood had gripped the nation, and although halfway across the world a bitter war continued against the Japanese, there were those who could not wait for what they saw as the inevitable surrender. Several days before VJ-Day, a huge crowd of sailors and civilians gathered for a celebration bonfire outside Portsmouth Post Office on the corner of Stanhope Road and Commercial Road. It was a wild repetition of VE night, with pub doors and furniture carried away to fuel the blaze, their windows smashed, and passing buses hit by bricks and missiles. Although the crowd was said to be good-humoured, police and naval patrols were kept busy, and an attempt to start another bonfire in Guildhall Square was quickly stopped. One pub manageress who saw her settees, chairs, fixtures, and doors piled on to the fire told a reporter: "I could not go through this kind of thing again. I would rather have the bombs."

When the official announcement of the Japanese surrender came at midnight on August 14, Portsmouth greeted the news with sirens, hooters, rockets, fireworks, bell ringing, singing and dancing. Sailors, soldiers, airmen and civilians thronged Guildhall Square until the small hours, and one group of ratings clambered to the precarious bell tower to ring out the Pompey chimes once again. At Southsea, residents and visitors marched arm in arm to the Common singing "Rule Britannia" and, according to newspaper reports, "making whoopee in an orderly way." The following night, thousands gathered around the three official bonfires at Southsea Common, Portsdown Hill, and Great Salterns, while scores of smaller fires burned in side streets and on waste land. There was only one disappointment. Almost every pub carried a chalked notice reading either "Closed" or "Sold Out." By the third night, the crowds were still singing and dancing in Guildhall Square, although the flagpoles which ratings had climbed on the first night had now been greased to stop any further antics, and the ladders to the Guildhall bell tower had been removed.

Gradually the celebrations faded and the country got back to the awesome task of winning the peace. No one was under any illusions. They knew it would be an uphill struggle, and this was reinforced in September when the Prime Minister, Mr. Clement Attlee, told the T.U.C. that he could hold out no hope of great improvements in the near future. In place of the blood, sweat and tears which Winston Churchill had promised war-time Britain came a call for patience, hard work, and co-operation. Not everyone was prepared to heed the call. Years of shortages had given rise to an inevitable black market which had been given plenty of practice at beating the system. A typical example arose in that first post-war autumn, when divisional C.I.D. headquarters at Fareham were on the track of a gang of racketeers who had been flooding the country with forged petrol coupons. For the vast majority of people, however, the war-time policy of thrift and "make do and mend" dragged on into peace-time and a new word was born — austerity. It was used to describe everything from meals to clothes and furniture, and it came to symbolise the period which lasted until the end of rationing in the early Fifties.

While there was little the people could do about austerity, there were other battles they could win, however small. As far as Portsmouth was concerned, it was adding insult to injury when the Dockyard continued to use its air-raid sirens as time signals for the work force. No one wanted to be reminded of that dreadful wailing note after all the city had endured, and there was an official protest in the House of Commons on August 22 when Major Sir Jocelyn Lucas, M.P. for Portsmouth South, told the First Lord of the Admiralty that the practice was causing "great annoyance and distress" to the city. He was assured that factory hooters would be installed as soon as they could be obtained, and the Evening News commented: "So we shall soon hear no more of 'Moaning Minnie', and citizens throughout the city who have been perturbed by its shrill screeching will be relieved." There were other more unpleasant reminders of the war years. Wicked gales in October washed ashore a crop of mines in the Portsmouth Command area, and mine disposal squads from H.M.S. Vernon were kept busy all along the coast from Hastings to the Devon border. The south-west shore of the Isle of Wight was a particular danger point, and at one stage was reported to be "littered" with mines torn loose by the gale, with reports of new ones coming in so fast that the authorities were hard pressed to keep track of them. Several exploded in unfrequented parts of the coast, and one particularly heavy detonation was felt in Freshwater and Yarmouth, where windows were broken. At Hayling, three mines were washed on to the beach but were dealt with by a police sergeant and a constable, who realised that the Navy had more than enough on their hands. By the time the gales had blown themselves out, Portsmouth Command had dealt with almost 100 mines, 20 of which had detonated on their own, fortunately with little damage.

In the peaceful countryside a few miles inland, there was an even more sombre reminder of the war. More than 200 child refugees from the notorious Nazi concentration camp at Belsen arrived at Durley, near Bishop's Waltham, in November to be cared for by the Jewish Refugee Committee. Aged between four and 17, they were housed at Winters Hill Hall, which had been war-time regional headquarters of the National Fire Service. A journalist who visited them reported: "Many of the children bear unmistakeable signs of ill-treatment, but they are intensely interested in everything around them and are being helped to forget the horrors they left behind. Some were born in captivity, and a concentration camp is the only "home" they have known. This is their first experience of kindness and comfort."

For these bewildered young people, Hampshire must have been a haven, however strange. For thousands of others who were coming back to these shores, it was quite simply home. There were tears in more than a few eyes on a grey and drizzling morning in November when the 35,000-ton battleship H.M.S. Nelson, manned almost entirely by Portsmouth men, steamed into harbour after eight months in the Far East. With the Royal Marines band playing stirring music as the huge ship tied up at South Railway Jetty, crew members threw bananas and oranges to children and relations in the waiting crowd. One sailor waved another prized item which had symbolised luxury in war-time Britain — a pair of silk panties. Another exotic cargo on its way to the city was delayed by bad weather. As a Christmas present, the people of South Africa had given half a million plum puddings to Great Britain, to be shared out among those towns and cities which had suffered particular hardsip during the war. Portsmouth was earmarked to receive 1,344 of them, but stormy weather meant that they missed the festive tables. There was also an acute shortage of coal, and householders were urged to exercise strict economy while keeping the home fires burning. It was a bleak Christmas all round. Gales were once again lashing the South Coast, and there were fresh reports of mines washed up from Brighton to Littlehampton, with squads from H.M.S. Vernon on standby over the holiday. The gales caused another problem for visitors on their way to the Isle of Wight. No steamers could sail because of the weather, and 1,400 people had to spend the night before Christmas Eve in a train at Portsmouth Harbour Station. Others slept on board S.S. Ryde at her moorings, and a further 200 toured the city searching for beds. Fortunately the wind dropped on Christmas Eve and the weary crowd were eventually shuttled across the Solent. Mountainous seas soon built up again, however, causing severe damage at Hayling Island, where several beach bungalows were wrecked and the billiards room at the Residential Club at Eastoke washed into the sea. Leave trains for naval personnel were cancelled when heavy rain undermined the track between Portsmouth and Guildford, and cross-Solent and cross-Channel ferry services were again halted.

There was one bright spot in the gloom, however. Four days after Christmas, it was announced that the first cargo of bananas to reach this country since 1940 was expected at Avonmouth Docks by the New Year. To the modern generation, it must seem inconceivable that such a mundane event could cause excitement. Yet to a nation which had gone without so much for so long, it was enough to guarantee a full civic welcome from Bristol's Lord Mayor. They were unlikely symbols of peace and hope, but those bananas meant that life, however slowly, was beginning to return to normal.

A pre-war view of Commercial Road, Portsmouth, looking towards the Guildhall, the tower of which can just be seen in the background. The Landport Drapery Bazaar is in the foreground, with the Bedford Hotel just behind it.

Kings Road, Southsea, at the beginning of 1945 — once a prosperous and busy shopping centre, now a wasteland awaiting redevelopment.

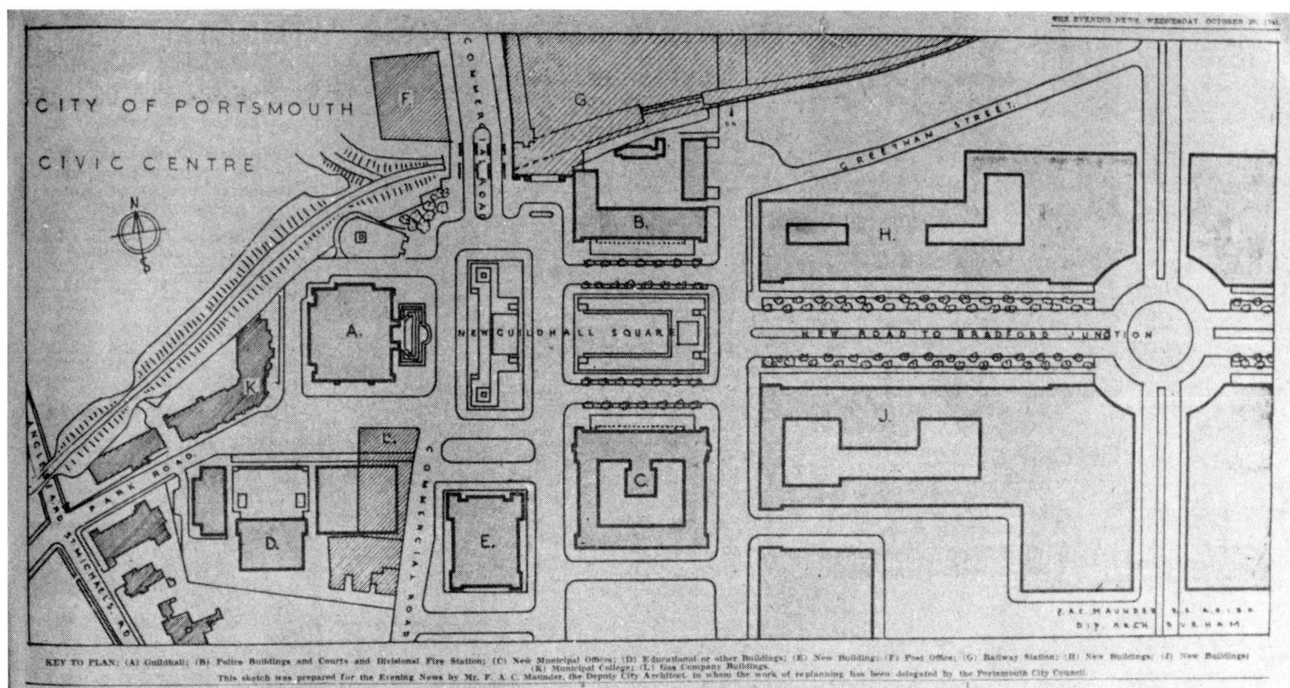

*One view of the proposed post-war Portsmouth, drawn up in 1944. The Guildhall, shown marked **A,** faces the gardens of a new Guildhall Square and a tree-lined avenue which leads to Bradford Junction. The area marked **F** is the Post Office, **G** the railway station, and **B** would have been a police station, fire station, and courts. New municipal offices were to be housed in the area marked **C.** Those marked **E, H and J** were simply designated as "new buildings."*

This was to be the face of post-war Portsmouth, according to an ambitious model which went on display in 1944. Councillors had been discussing the scheme as early as the autumn of 1941, nine months after the Guildhall had been reduced to a smoking ruin. A special committee charged with replanning the city envisaged rebuilding the Guildhall as a Mansion House, with a huge open square in front and various civic departments surrounding it. A processional road would have led to Bradford Junction, and from there to Eastern Road and Hayling. Some councillors thought the plan premature in 1941, others wanted housing put first, but the rebirth of the city centre was seen as a morale booster. When the council met at the Royal Beach Hotel, Southsea, on October 28, 1941, only three members voted in favour of postponing the subject until the war was over.

Women brick cleaners busy salvaging serviceable materials from the rubble of war. Huge numbers of such bricks were put by for use in rebuilding the shattered city, as shown by the dump ***(below)*** *in Conway Street, Landport.*

Firemen from the squad which rebuilt Somers Road fire station from the rubble of war, using old bricks for the inner skins and new ones from Rowlands Castle for the facing.

The fighting over for them, German prisoners-of-war were put to work helping with the reconstruction of the towns their countrymen had blitzed. This group are pictured on a housing estate at Gosport.

The First Lord of the Admiralty, Mr. Brendan Bracken ***(above)*** *gets a first-hand look at a captured German E-boat in Portsmouth Harbour. The first two, one of which is pictured below, caused quite a stir when they arrived at H.M.S. Hornet, the coastal forces base at Gosport, at the tail end of the war.*

Crew members from captured E-boats, once the scourge of the Channel, arrive in captivity at Gosport in the summer of 1945.

This captured German Tiger Tank was put to good use at Victoria Barracks, Portsmouth, when it went on show as part of a Savings Week Exhibition. The war may have been over, but thrift was still to be the watchword for several years.

A time to rejoice as the liner Corfu brings home to Southampton the first repatriated prisoners-of-war from the Far East on October 7, 1945. As they landed, each man was given a message from the King, cigarettes, chocolate, and a form for a free telegram to their homes.

The Yanks go home — the Stars and Stripes come down at the R.A.O.C. depot at Hilsea in July, 1945, as the U.S. Army officially hands it back to the British. A key installation during the build-up to D-Day, it had 4,000 Servicemen working there in the spring and summer of 1944, handling food and clothing for 90,000 troops. ***Below, right:*** *How the Evening News reported the end of the war.*

The Evening News AND SOUTHERN DAILY MAIL. VICTORY EDITION

ONE PENNY.

PORTSMOUTH & SOUTHSEA. MONDAY, MAY 7, 1945

MORE EGGS

A1 The finest cooking date

Mr. CHURCHILL PRESIDING AT A FULL MEETING OF CABINET

"WE HAVE SUCCUMBED" SAYS GERMAN FOREIGN MINISTER

TOTAL SURRENDER

DOENITZ ORDER MEANS END OF WAR IN EUROPE

DOENITZ has ordered the unconditional surrender of all German fighting troops. Earlier he had ordered the U-boats to cease activity, and Allied - controlled Danish radio had reported the capitulation of the Germans in Norway. The formal VE-Day statement is expected hourly.

LAST RATION THE WAR

London Puts Up Flags

PATTON'S ADVANCE ON PRAGUE

Guildhall Square was the scene for many war-time gatherings from the outbreak of war to the first days of peace. This photograph was taken from the steps on May 26, 1940, when thousands joined in a service of national prayer. Five years later, a more boisterous crowd celebrated VE-Day in the Square by burning almost anything they could get their hands on.

Its deadly hail silenced, the rocket battery on Southsea Common packs up in June, 1945.

With the Channel Isles liberated from the Germans in May, 1945, the King and Queen pass through Portsmouth on their way to visit the islands one month later, on the anniversary of D-Day. They were due to fly there, but bad weather forced them to transfer to the cruiser H.M.S. Jamaica.

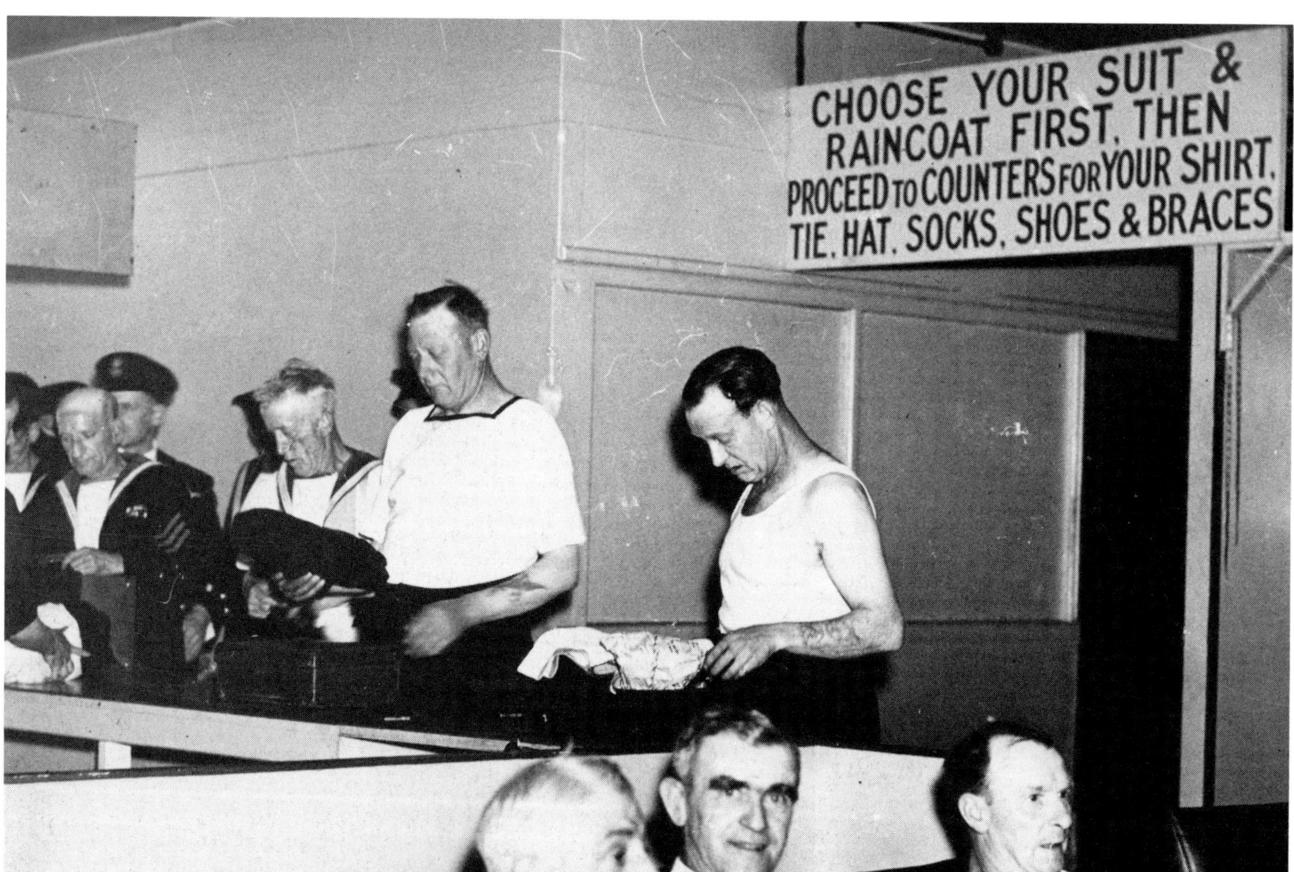

Old salts line up to exchange Navy blue for civilian grey or brown at the demobilisation clothing centre at Cosham in June, 1945. Every man was given a complete outfit, from raincoat to collar studs and cufflinks, and the centre boasted that it could kit a Serviceman out for Civvy Street in 15 minutes.

Two ways to relax. ***Above:*** *A Royal Artillery birthday party — complete with elaborately iced cake — just one month after war broke out, before rationing had begun to bite.* ***Below:*** *A portable wind-up gramophone provided the entertainment for this group of R.A.O.C. volunteers.*

Smiling through the traditional Army chore of "spud-bashing", this group of soldiers put a brave face on their potato-peeling fatigues.

Thankfully, some bombs fell harmlessly wide of their intended targets and became subjects of mere curiosity. This one made a mess of the countryside at Hambledon in September, 1940.

The wheel comes full circle. This photograph was taken at Fratton in February, 1940, when a fuel shortage plagued the country during intensely cold weather. Five years later, the story was exactly the same, with long queues waiting patiently for their precious coal ration.

Dukws — amphibious troop carriers — wait to embark at Gosport at the end of 1944, bound for France. Huge quantities of arms, material, and men had been funnelled through Portsmouth during the eventful months on either side of D-Day.

On its way to join the big push after D-Day, a Churchill tank is loaded at Hardway, Gosport, in July, 1944.

Exchanging one uniform for another, these homecoming sailors swop navy blue for the regulation demob raincoat.

But will it fit? An apprehensive looking ex-matelot gets a helping hand as he tries tilting his new trilby.

How do I look, girls? A former leading stoker gives admiring Wrens a glimpse of the Civvy Street look.

The transformation — for some — is complete as they face the camera and a sometimes bewildering new world in the summer of 1945.